102
Powerful, Gripping and Intriguing
Ideas for Thriller Writers

102
Powerful, Gripping and Intriguing
Ideas for Thriller Writers

Dave Haslett

ideas4writers

Published in Great Britain in 2017

by

ideas4writers
2a New Street
Cullompton
Devon
EX15 1HA

www.ideas4writers.co.uk

Other books in this series

Genre Fiction:

- 189 Seriously Good Ideas for **Comedy** Writers
- 215 Arrestingly Good Ideas for Writing Captivating **Crime** Stories
- 78 Brain-Stimulating Ideas for **Erotica** Writers
- 139 Practical and Imaginative Ideas for **Fantasy** Writers
- 92 Practical Ideas for Writing Authentic **Historical** Fiction
- 106 Frightfully Good Ideas for **Horror** Writers
- 87 Crafty, Compelling and Clued-up Ideas for **Mystery and Suspense** Writers
- 176 Lovingly Crafted Ideas for **Romance** Writers
- 122 Down-to-Earth Ideas for **Science Fiction** Writers
- 102 Powerful, Gripping and Intriguing ideas for **Thriller** Writers

The Elements of Fiction:

- 377 Ideas for Creating Memorable and Compelling **Characters**
- 94 Ideas for Writing Vivid and Evocative **Descriptions and Settings**
- 138 Ideas for Writing Dazzling and Authentic **Dialogue**
- 109 Ideas for Writing Better and More Dramatic **Plots**
- 81 Ideas for Adding **Strength and Structure** to Your Writing
- 21 Ideas for Identifying and Strengthening **Themes** in Your Writing

General Fiction:

- 394 Ideas for **Fiction** Writers: Create Unique, Compelling and Successful Stories Faster and Easier than Ever Before
- 192 Essential and Inspiring Ideas for Writing Bestselling **Novels**
- 87 Creativity-Boosting Ideas for Budding **Screenwriters**
- 65 Curtain-Raising Ideas for Writing Your First **Stage Play**
- 234 Easy Ideas for Successful **Short Stories** You Can Sell
- 125 Ready-to-Use **Storylines** to Instantly Inspire Writers

Practical Matters:

- 117 Painless, Efficient and Awesome Ideas for **Editing** and Strengthening Your Writing
- 218 Innovative and Inspiring Ways to Find Writing **Ideas**
- 128 Simple, Practical and Indispensable Ideas for **Getting Your Writing Published**
- 30 Confidence-Boosting Ideas for **Overcoming Rejection** and Getting Published
- 75 Money-Spinning Ideas for **Self-Publishing and Marketing** Your Writing
- 143 Smashing Ideas for Crushing Your **Writer's Block**
- 159 Creative and Inspiring **Ideas for Writers**

Children, YA, Nonfiction, Poetry, Travel:

- 201 Imaginative and Inspiring Ideas for **Children's Writers**
- 73 Creative and Inspiring Ideas for **Young Adult/Teen Writers**
- 301 Cut-Out-and-Keep Ideas for Writing **Magazine Articles**
- 160 Creative and Inspiring Ideas for **Nonfiction** Writers

- 125 Essential and Vers(e)atile Ideas for Writing **Poetry**
- 75 Worldly-Wise Ideas for **Travel** Writers

Introduction

Welcome, thriller writers!

Within this book you'll find more than 102 powerful, gripping and intriguing ideas to inspire characters, stories, situations and locations. We've even given you some instant, ready-made storylines that you can base your own scenes and stories on.

You'll also find plenty of insider tips and expert advice to help you improve your writing, write faster, get your work published, and much more.

You're welcome to use these ideas exactly as we've written them, or you can adapt them in any way that you wish. For example, you could use them as a starting point for your own ideas, and let your imagination wander. That could lead to your own cast of unique and individual characters, brand new stories, and all sorts of interesting and exotic locations to thrill your readers.

Although the ideas generally refer to the protagonist and villain as male, that needn't be the case. They would work equally well (or perhaps ever better) if either or both characters were female.

Don't forget to check out the other books in this series. We have tons of great ideas to help you improve your writing skills and craft, edit your work, sell and market it, overcome writer's block and rejection, find a publisher, or publish your books yourself, and much more.

Our collection of travel ideas might be just the thing if you want to set your stories in foreign lands.

And, of course, the thriller genre itself spans multiple sub-genres. If you're interested in writing a comedy thriller, for example, you'll definitely want to have a look at our collection of comedy ideas. On the other hand, if romantic thrillers are more your cup of tea, we have romance ideas too. Or how about historical thrillers? We have a terrific collection of historical ideas. Thrillers in space? Or in the future? Or in an alternative universe? Check out our collection of science fiction ideas! I'm sure you get the idea.

The thriller genre is huge and wonderfully versatile. You can combine the ideas in this book with those from any of the other genres. And that will give you an endless, unlimited supply of brilliant ideas for fresh new characters and intriguing and unusual plots that will leave your readers wanting more.

And that's a good thing, because not only are thrillers one of the most popular genres in the world, but the novels that sell best are the ones that form part of a series. So the more ideas you have, the more books you can write – and the more money you can make!

Good luck!

And happy, successful, and profitable writing!

Part 1: Ideas

1. A death on every page

How about writing a thriller that has a death on every page? That's a heck of a commitment, but it gives you a fairly straightforward structure for your story.

As well as a whole string of deaths – perhaps 250 or more – you'll also need a decent storyline, and maybe a couple of sub-plots too. Some of the deaths might occur in the main plot, and some in the sub-plots.

You won't be able to spend an entire page covering each death, otherwise you won't have any room left for the story. So some of the victims will have to be disposed of in just a line or two. Some of the deaths might happen off the page and be reported rather than witnessed. Some might pass virtually unnoticed.

But if you kill one of your main characters, or someone close to a main character, you'll need to cover that in more detail, and give the surviving characters time and space to grieve. That particular death, and its repercussions, might go on for several pages or be referred to in several of the subsequent chapters. Meanwhile, other people – the more minor characters – continue to die at the steady rate of one per page – including the very last page.

They don't all have to be murdered, of course. There might be accidents, illnesses, suicides, overdoses, stillbirths, natural deaths from old age, and all sorts of mysterious and bizarre circumstances that might or not be resolved later in the book. Some of them might not be what they first appear.

This story could work well as a comedy-thriller. You could even call it "A Death on Every Page." But it's important to keep in mind that the published book will have page breaks in different places than your manuscript. You might like to choose a published novel and set the page size, margins and font in your word processor to match. If you'll be working with a publisher, be sure to mention this in your covering letter.

2. Against the clock 1

There's no easier way of adding tension to a thriller than by introducing a time limit that your readers are aware of.

Examples might include a timer on a bomb, a clock counting down to zero, or a race against an (almost) impossible deadline.

If someone has been kidnapped, set a deadline by which the ransom must be paid. If someone has borrowed money from the mob, set a deadline by which it has to be repaid or they'll break the borrower's legs. If a company is struggling financially, set a deadline by which sufficient funds have to be raised before the bank pulls the plug. The struggling company might even be your detective's own business. If someone is bleeding to death and they can't stop it, keep the reader informed of how much time the victim has left.

Sometimes, your hero might not know what the deadline is. He might have several hours, or he might only have a few minutes. But the ticking clock will always be on his mind – and also on your readers' minds.

Once you've set up the event and introduced the ticking clock, you just need to add a whole heap of obstacles designed to prevent your hero from meeting the deadline, and severely stress him out. Usually, he'll make the deadline in the nick of time. But that doesn't always have to be the case.

> [EXTENSION] You can raise the stakes by suddenly and dramatically shortening the deadline. Your hero thought he had hours, but something has gone seriously wrong, and now he only has minutes.
>
> Perhaps he cut the wrong wire while defusing the bomb, and the timer jumped forward by several hours. Perhaps he's upset the kidnappers or the moneylenders, and they've changed the deadline. Perhaps the person he's driving to the hospital has stopped breathing. Your hero was already under pressure, but now he's in serious trouble. And he might not operate at his best when he's under that much stress. He might make mistakes or bad decisions, or not pay as much attention to something as he should do.
>
> On the other hand, stressful situations might bring out the best in him. They give you the opportunity to show your readers what he's really made of. And that might be why they love your stories so much.

3. Against the clock 2

To keep the suspense going, it's a good idea to keep reminding your readers of the time. A common way of doing this is to state the time and date at the start of each scene. But as time runs out, and the deadline nears, it's better to switch formats and state the amount of time remaining instead. This has much more impact, and your readers don't have to stop to work out how long your hero has left to solve the problem.

Most readers will hardly notice the switch, but they'll register it subconsciously, and their anxiety levels will rise – which is exactly the effect you're looking for.

4. Against the clock 3

What if the villain shortens the deadline? He might even do this several times. It could be his way of punishing your hero after he makes a failed attempt to capture him or rescue the victim. Not only was your hero thwarted, but a significant amount of time was knocked off the deadline. Now he has less time to carry out his daring mission, and that means he's under even more pressure.

5. Being chased

Can you remember a time when you were being chased? Perhaps the school bully was after you. Or you'd broken someone's window, and the owner was chasing you up the street. Or you'd stolen apples from a tree. Or you'd beaten up a little kid, and his big brother was after you. If you think back to your childhood, you'll probably remember several such instances. See if you can remember what it felt like.

It's even better if you've been chased as an adult, because your memory of the event will be clearer. The danger was probably greater too.

Did your panic give you extra speed? Did the adrenalin rush give your pursuer extra speed too? Did it feel like a life-or-death situation? Were you able to get away? Or hide? Or lead him into a trap? Or did he catch you? If you got caught, what happened?

You can put these incidents and emotions and the sense of panic into your thriller to give it an added feeling of realism: the thrill of the chase.

During the chase scene, it's a good idea to make the person being chased the viewpoint character, even if they're not the main character in the story. This will allow him to report everything that happens, second by second. It will create a lively, dramatic scene and your readers will be on tenterhooks as they follow the action and wait to see if he escapes.

Of course, in your story, your hero probably won't be chased for such a trivial thing as a broken window or a few stolen apples. It might actually be a life-or-death situation. Whether or not he gets caught is up to you. But if he does, he'll be in serious trouble.

6. Bombs – actual or metaphorical

Every good thriller needs a bomb. It doesn't have to be an actual bomb (but it could be). It might be an explosive situation, such as a boss who lets rip at an employee who's screwed up. Or it might happen inside one of your characters' heads – an explosion of rage, for example – which could be the turning point of the story. Or, of course, the explosion in his head might be a physical thing: a medical emergency such as a burst blood vessel. Or it might be caused by a gunshot.

There are two important characteristics of a bomb that we need to capture (even if it's not an actual bomb):

- a slow-burning fuse that adds tension

- a massive explosion that rips everything apart and changes the rest of the story forever

There might be several bombs in your story. Your hero might manage to defuse a few of them to begin with. But then there's a big one. He might manage to stop it just in the nick of time, but it'll be much more difficult than any of the others he's encountered. Or, despite his best efforts, the bomb might explode.

As he's the hero of the story, he (probably) won't get killed. But other people might. It might just shake him up. Or, if people he cares about, or their property, have been harmed, he might feel distraught and angry with himself. If only he'd managed to stop the bomb from exploding, he might have prevented all this carnage. But did he really have any hope of stopping it anyway? Is he beating himself up over something that could never have succeeded?

What happens when the "bomb" explodes? Will he stop to help people? Or will he run for his life?

Perhaps the person that everyone thought was the hero runs away, while the real hero risks his life by staying behind to help. That might be the moment when we learn who the true hero of the story is.

What happens afterward? How will the story have changed?

7. Business rivals

You could write a thriller about two (or more) rival businesses that are chasing the same customer or contract and will stop at nothing to get it.

The stakes are high. The winning business could be saved from bankruptcy, and all its employees will keep their jobs. They might even get bonuses - which some of them may be desperate for or depending on.

For the losers though, it might mean the end of their company. They might even get taken over by the winning company, and some of their staff might transfer across to work alongside their former rivals. (Will they still regard them as their enemies? Or their saviors?) Or they might have to find some other industry to work in.

It might all be too much for some of the losers. Perhaps they sank everything they had into their company, and now it's gone. They might decide that life is no longer worth living. Will you save them? Will you have them rescue someone and save the day, proving that they have something to live for after all? Or will you give them a shocking demise?

Perhaps they decide that if they're going down, they're taking others with them. And the people they're taking with them might be the competitors that beat them to the contract.

8. Characters – real

How about including a real person in your story? If you get this right, it can give your readers goosebumps!

Find an autobiography or an authorized biography of a well-known person – ideally, it should be a book that contains one or more shocking revelations. Choose one (or more) of those revelations, and include the real person and their shocking event in your story.

Perhaps one of your characters witnessed the event, or took part in it, or was the first to discover it, or was affected by it.

You can't libel the real-life person because he has already admitted it in his book. But it's important that when you describe the event in your own book, you stick to the facts as they were described in the biography, and don't alter them.

Including this person in your story will make it seem much more real, and the events will seem more shocking. Many of your readers will pore over the details avidly, even if you don't reveal anything more than was revealed in the biography.

Hopefully, some of the more lurid details didn't make it into the press at the time of the event, or when the biography was published. Your readers might learn about the event, and some of the more shocking details, for the first time when they read your book.

If the person is well known, but the full, shocking details of the event aren't widely known, you could use it as a fantastic way of generating publicity for your own book.

9. Characters – scary

For a thrilling story, include a character that you're scared to write about. If he scares you, the writer, just think what effect he'll have on your readers, who don't know what's going to happen next.

- Perhaps your scary character is unpredictable or excessively violent, especially towards those who can't defend themselves.

- Perhaps his punishments are so cruel that they should be classed as torture – and extreme torture at that.

- Perhaps it takes six men to hold him down – if there are only five of them, they're in serious trouble.

- Perhaps his mind is so warped and twisted that he's basically a wild animal or a demon.

- Perhaps he seems perfectly ordinary to most people … until they see his scary side, or learn about the things he's done. And then they're so scared that they're violently sick.

See what other ideas you can come up with to create the character of your nightmares (and everyone else's).

10. Conspiracy theories

There are always plenty of interesting conspiracy theories around to base your stories on. They're widely featured in newspapers (especially the tabloids), and countless TV documentaries are made about them. There are plenty of books and websites about them too. Just type "conspiracy theories" into any search engine and see what turns up. Or read the newspapers after any significant event. Or pick a significant event from history and look through the newspaper archives to see what sort of outlandish theories were proposed afterward.

> [TIP] It's well worth keeping an eye on the cable and satellite documentary channels, especially History, Discovery and Science. Conspiracy theories make up a significant part of their output. If you aren't able to access the channels, at least visit or subscribe to their websites so you get updates and announcements about their latest shows. You can then try to find out more about them, or discuss them in forums and Facebook groups with people who watched them. They'll give you a wealth of material for your stories.

[ALTERNATIVE] Another approach is to make up your own conspiracy theory. I recommend learning about other conspiracy theories first. You need to get a feel for how they work so that yours will sound plausible – or, at the very least, possible.

11. Countdowns

Many thrillers use countdowns to raise the tension. When we think of countdowns we usually think of time: a ticking clock, the timer on a bomb, and so on. But there are other types of countdown that you might not have considered.

You could do it with people: you might start out with a large gang, but kill them all off one by one until there's only one left. Similarly, you could take out soldiers or guards one at a time.

Or you could do it with vehicles: there might be many at the beginning of the scene or story, but very few left by the end.

Other countdown possibilities might include weapons, ammunition and escape routes. Can you think of any more?

You could also combine different forms of countdown to really put your characters under pressure. For example:

- time is running out
- their ammunition is running out
- they're running out of places to hide
- their vehicles are being damaged, destroyed or captured
- their fuel is running out

- key members of their team keep going missing, getting killed, or are too injured to continue

You can show each type of countdown slowly (or quickly) declining over the course of the scene or story.

Imagine how your hero feels by the end. He might be the only one left standing, he's got the last functioning vehicle but hardly any fuel, only one path he can take, and only a single bullet left. And there's still the small matter of the bomb that's about to explode … any second now.

12. Customs and border checks

It can be interesting – and educational – to spend a day in the arrivals area of an international airport or ferry terminal. Just sit and watch the people coming through. They're getting ready to go through the customs checks. Some of them will act suspiciously. Perhaps they're just nervous. Perhaps they're carrying something illegal. Will the customs officers stop them? Would you stop them if you were a customs officer? What about the people who act "confident" and breeze through, seemingly without a care. They're just as likely to be smuggling something as the nervous ones, they might just be better at it. Which of them would you stop and search?

You'll need to contact the customs officers at the place where you'd like to carry out your observations, to ask if you can do this. And why not ask if you could spend a day with them? Tell them you're researching a book: that's usually enough to secure their agreement. When you get there, ask them to explain what they're looking for, why they let certain people through and stop others, and so on. You'll be amazed at what you learn. You'll be able to include authentic background details and descriptions of the sights and sounds and processes in your stories. It's also a terrific source of plot and character ideas.

If they won't let you spend a day with them, try again somewhere else. Or just go along and watch them anyway: but try not to get arrested for loitering or acting suspiciously. If they ask you what you're doing there, you can either tell them you're researching a book – and maybe show them a copy of the letter or email you sent them when you first asked – or you could say you're waiting for someone who missed their boat or plane. Either way, the worst that will happen is that they'll ask you to leave.

Another option is to watch TV shows about the real-life customs and border control officers. There are plenty of these shows – just about every TV channel has one. The slight drawback is that they all tend to focus on the travelers who have been stopped – most of them for good reason. You rarely get to see the ones they don't stop, nor do you get any explanation about why they weren't stopped. That's why real-life observation, and spending a day with the officers, is always better if you can arrange it.

13. Disasters 1

A disaster always makes a good basis for a story. People are under just about as much stress as they can bear. Emotions run high. Tempers flare. Brains are on overdrive. Delays seem to take forever. This is a time for heroes to make themselves known and show the world what they're really made of. And the world depends on their success.

There are hundreds of different types of disaster, and you could easily spend a couple of hours or more just listing them all and picking an interesting one to write about. But you don't have to stop at one: why not write a series, each based on a different one? In each case, you could choose a real-life incident or make up one of your own.

There are plenty of disasters you could consider, both natural and man-made. Here are just a few examples:

- drought
- famine
- chemical or nuclear leak
- forest fire
- radiation from space
- landslide
- train wreck
- multi-vehicle car crash
- volcano
- a new ice age
- heat wave
- and many more

I would tend to avoid sinking ships, meteor strikes, floods, skyscraper fires, and space-related disasters for now, as they've filled the market in recent years. But if you can come up with something genuinely original then, by all means, choose one of them.

> [TIP] Remember to let the tension build gradually. Perhaps a monitoring device has picked up something out of the ordinary. No one is particularly concerned to begin with; it might just be another false alarm or a calibration error. Someone might comment that the anomalies seem to be happening more often. They might

wonder whether the sensor needs replacing, because there can't *really* be anything wrong. That would be unthinkable...

14. Disasters 2

Think of an important moment in history: a disaster, especially a man-made one. Ideally, pick one where no one knew the incident was about to happen (apart from the villains, if there were any). You can use this as the basis for your story.

But your version of it might be very different. Let's say that your hero knew what was about to happen, and he was working frantically behind the scenes to prevent it. Since the incident actually happened, we know he must have failed. But we don't know the story behind his failure: the amazing heroics that took place, the astonishing bravery, the small chance that he might succeed, and the disbelief and despair when it all went wrong.

You should be able to find plenty of information about the real-life disaster from books, newspaper archives, and websites. All you have to do is insert your hero into the story, but keep him out of public view behind the scenes.

How did he find out about the impending disaster? What made him want to do something about it? Perhaps he tried to alert the authorities, but failed to convince them of the seriousness of what could happen. Perhaps he thought there was no need to bother the authorities, as he could sort it out himself. Or perhaps it was the authorities that called upon him to fix it – with strict instructions not to tell anyone else what was going on.

15. Double pursuits

Double pursuits can make your story more thrilling: your hero is chasing someone while he's being chased by someone else.

He knows he's being chased – and he's desperate to avoid being caught. But he's equally desperate to catch up with whoever he's chasing. This scene might only last for a few minutes – but what an exciting few minutes!

What if he catches up with whoever he's chasing? Presumably, he'll have to stop and deal with the situation. But if he's still being chased by someone who means him harm, he won't want to stop. That makes an interesting dilemma!

16. Drama!

As you write each scene in your story, try to make it as dramatic as it can possibly be. Start with your original idea for that scene, and then ask yourself: how can I make this more dramatic? Repeat that process five or even ten times, increasing the level of drama by a notch or two each time.

What might start out as a *fairly* dramatic scene will become an *enormously* dramatic scene. Do this for every scene in your story that features some drama, and you'll turn a regular thriller into a dramatic masterpiece.

Don't do this in every scene in your story, though. You need to allow your readers (and your characters) occasional moments of respite and reflection.

But don't give your characters quite enough time to think things through and make proper plans. Plunge them into the next dramatic scene before they've got things worked out. They might have the vague outline or beginning of a plan, but they'll have to make up the details as they go along, and adapt on the fly as the situation changes. That'll show your readers what they're made of!

17. Emergency

Think about a time in your life when there was an emergency.

Perhaps someone was injured, and you needed to find help or take them to the hospital or look after them until an ambulance arrived.

Perhaps you came home and there was a burglary in progress. You called the police and had to wait for them to arrive, while listening to the sounds of smashing glass and splintering wood coming from inside your house.

Perhaps there was a fire, and there was nothing you could do but wait for the emergency services to arrive.

See if you can recall the exact circumstances: the cause, the effect, how it affected you, what you did, and how it affected others. Was there anything more you could have done? Do you wish you had done something differently? Do you feel regretful? Do you feel responsible for any part of what happened?

These are strong, authentic feelings, and they'll add a great deal of impact to your story.

You might change the circumstances, either because you find it too upsetting to write about, or because it would make the story more dramatic. For example, you might have witnessed a particular building on fire, but write a scene where it's a different building or even a car that's on fire.

Remember how you felt, and have your main character feel the exact same thing: the tension, the anxiety, the fear, the sense of urgency, the sense of frustration – all with the same level of intensity as you did.

Even though you're writing fiction, you'll be writing much of this scene from memory, so the words should come quickly and easily.

> [NOTE] You might relive the original incident in your mind with even more intensity than you did when it occurred. Be prepared for this: it might affect your more than you think.

18. Endings – kidnapping

I was asked how I would end a thriller in which kidnappers take people hostage. How would I give it a thrilling climax? Here's one of the ideas I came up with:

The police appear to give in to the kidnappers' demands. They publish fake news stories, video footage, and recordings of phone calls that appear to show the villains' demands being met. They send in the helicopter that the villains requested: it'll take them wherever they want to go. The villains abandon the hostages and climb aboard the helicopter. To make doubly sure the villains leave the hostages behind, there's only enough room on board for the villains.

But the helicopter is being flown by remote control, the controls have been disabled, and the pilot is a dummy. (If you're writing a sci-fi-thriller, the pilot could be a robot.)

As soon as the kidnappers are on board, the doors lock. The helicopter could now fly them straight to the police. But if the villains still have their weapons with them, that might not be a good idea.

So the helicopter could perform some aerobatic maneuvers to throw them about inside and injure them. Perhaps it flies out to sea or over a river, tilts onto its side, the doors open, the safety harnesses release, and the villains are dumped in the water.

Just in case any of them hold onto something to keep themselves from falling, they might receive a jolt of electricity to help them on their way.

The police rescue them from the water, and they're arrested. The helicopter returns to base, mission accomplished. And the hostages are recovered, safe and sound.

Would you do it differently?

19. Fake medics

You occasionally hear worrying reports about doctors, nurses, and surgeons who've been practicing medicine for years but aren't actually qualified. That could make an excellent thriller. Ask the usual questions to get started: who, why, what, how, when and where?

How many rogue doctors, nurses or surgeons will you have in your story? You might only have one. But it could be a pair that work in collusion, or even a group of them.

Let's consider the group idea. Do they know each other? Do they know that their colleagues aren't qualified? Perhaps they refer patients to each other. Are they trying to make people's lives better? Do they succeed, or do they make things worse? Perhaps they deliberately cause suffering – or even death – but by working together, they can cover it up.

Who suffers as a result? Your story might feature patients and families whose lives have been ruined.

But the doctors might have faked other things too. Their personal relationships might be based on lies. Who becomes suspicious about them, and why? How do they get found out?

If you need some ideas, try researching a real-life case. You could even try interviewing someone who actually did it.

> [ALTERNATIVE] Perhaps, instead of writing a thriller, you could write a biography of the real-life fake doctor, or ghostwrite their autobiography. Use thriller-writing techniques to make it a gripping read that pulls readers along and has them on the edges of their seats.

20. Fakes

Write a thriller that revolves around a fake or forgery. What sort of fake will you choose? Perhaps one of these:

- artwork
- antiques
- banknotes or coins
- merchandise - CDs, DVDs, clothing, electrical goods, toys, etc.
- credit cards

- uniforms
- weapons or bombs
- watches
- drugs or medicines
- documents: invoices, passports, property deeds, stock holdings, and so on
- identities

Or perhaps the fakes are people. They might impersonate someone. For example, crooks might wear stolen (or fake) police uniforms or dress as officials who need access to your house. Someone with no qualifications might claim to be a university professor, a doctor, a therapist, or something else. Someone might claim to be a missing relative, perhaps arriving just in time to claim an inheritance.

You should be able to come up with lots more examples of these.

21. Feel the fear

One of the biggest secrets of successful thrillers is to really scare your readers. You want them to physically feel the fear – or, at the very least, to feel anxious and insecure. You shouldn't have any qualms about doing this; if this sort of thing upset them, they wouldn't be reading thrillers in the first place.

- Make them bite their fingernails to the bone as they frantically turn the pages, wondering what the heck is going to happen next.

- Make them have to sleep with their heads under the bedclothes, or leave the lights on all night, thanks to the images you've planted in their minds.

- Make them feel so insecure that they have to double-check all the doors and windows are locked before going to bed – and before picking up your book again to read the next chapter.

- Make them lie awake half the night listening out for the slightest noise and wondering what it might be.

- And all the while they'll be thinking about the characters in your story and worrying that it could happen to them.

Think about the experiences you've had that made you feel this way. Your job as a thriller writer is to recall exactly what it felt like. Think about the irrational thoughts it triggered and the things you did as a result. And then capture it all on the page as accurately and realistically as you possibly can.

You'll end up with a fantastic thriller that your readers will love. They'll talk about it for months afterward, which means even more people will buy it and talk about it.

22. Gadgets

If there's one thing everyone remembers about the James Bond books and movies, it's the gadgets. People love them. So how about inventing a few of your own?

They needn't be too outlandish. Some of James Bond's earliest gadgets, while fictional at the time, actually exist now. Decide what sort of sticky situations your hero is going to find himself in. Then do some lateral thinking to come up with interesting and unusual new gadgets that he could use to get himself out of trouble.

You should stay within the realms of science and plausibility. But jumping ahead 25 years or so and imagining what might be possible then is perfectly acceptable. Who knows what technology is being developed in secret labs right now? Some of it will become the gadgets of tomorrow. And some of it might be so secret that we never get to hear about it at all – or at least not until it's obsolete and has been replaced by something better.

> [EXTENSION] You could also write a spoof thriller that's all about using gadgets for the sake of it. Your "story" will have minimal plot and characterization, but lots and lots of unlikely gadgets, and endless opportunities to use them.
>
> In this type of story, you don't even have to stick to the limits of science or be bound by plausibility. You can make them as unlikely as you like. And if they happen to go wrong, well, that can be even funnier.

23. Heroes – apparently dead

What if your readers think your hero is dead? That will shock them. Killing your hero is easy; just have him cut the wrong wire or something. The hard part is bringing him back into the story again later. Because he didn't really die, of course. Actually killing your hero is rarely a good idea.

Finding a plausible way of bringing your hero back into the story can be enormously difficult. But if you get it just right, the effect can be shocking and amazing.

Many writers have attempted to bring "dead" heroes back, but few of them have done it well. So you'll need to spend a long time thinking about this. It needs to be simple, plausible and realistic. That rules out things like waking from a dream – or from someone else's dream, walking back into the room as if nothing had happened, or being cryogenically frozen and brought back to life centuries later.

24. Heroes – helpless

How about putting your hero in a position where he's completely helpless? And what if someone who's entirely innocent is about to kill him without realizing it? Here are some examples:

- The villain has captured your hero. Perhaps he's rendered him unconscious or paralyzed him in some way, dressed him in rags and a mask, and donated him to some children to burn on their bonfire for Guy Fawkes Night (Britain's fireworks night on November 5th).

- Or he might be dressed as some other effigy that people plan to burn – perhaps as a political protest.

- Perhaps he's been disguised as a crash test dummy.

- Perhaps he's a human-shaped target for weapons training.

Let's explore the crash test dummy example.

What if his friends finally track him down, and they demand that the test is halted? But they're too late. The high-speed cameras are already rolling, and the car he's strapped into is already heading towards a wall at high speed. There's no way of stopping it. Are they about to witness his sticky end? Probably not.

Perhaps it isn't your hero after all, but someone else. Who that person might be, and how he got there, is entirely up to you. It could be a good way of killing off one of your other characters. But why does everyone think it's your hero? And how did he escape?

Or perhaps it really *is* your hero in the car, but he survives the crash. They might be testing a new type of safety harness or passenger protection system. When they pull him out, he'll be unharmed – but absolutely furious.

Or perhaps your hero has somehow tricked the villain into taking his place in the car. That will require some clever talking!

What other situations can you think of where your hero is rendered helpless like this? Or where the villain backs off and leaves the killing to someone who has no idea anything is wrong?

25. Heroes – revealed at the end

Who is the hero of your story? What if you don't reveal who he is until the very end?

You'll need a group of good guys to fight the baddies. Choose one of the good guys as your viewpoint character and let him tell the story for a few chapters. Then you might have a dramatic scene in which he dies.

The next chapter will have a different character taking up the story – almost certainly another one of good guys. He'll be upset at the loss of his colleague and he'll want revenge. And so the fight goes on. But this guy will die in a few chapters' time too, and someone else will then take over telling the story.

The real hero will be the last one standing: the one who faces and defeats the bad guys all by himself. We'll see the dramatic climax through his eyes. And not only does he defeat the bad guys (possibly single-handed), he also avenges the death of the others – just as he may have promised earlier. He might even get the girl if you've included a romantic sub-plot.

Of course, this heroic character needs to have played a prominent role throughout the story. We can't have him just appearing out of nowhere at the end of the story because it's convenient for the writer.

You also shouldn't show him as a weakling throughout the story but suddenly make him super-strong at the end. If you're going to do that, you need to show him gaining strength, even if it's just a background detail that doesn't seem particularly important at the time.

For example, when the characters are talking about their day, he might say he's joined a gym. The others might even laugh about this because he's such a weedy little guy, and going to the gym seems so unlikely. Later, he might say things are going well and he now has a personal trainer, or is exploring martial arts, and so on. Or he might get laughed at for being the lousiest shot in the group, but then he mentions that he has joined a rifle club and is making rapid progress.

26. Jealousy

Jealousy is a strong negative emotion that can lead to all sorts of things: revenge, threats, blackmail, vandalism, theft, kidnapping, murder, and so on. These are all classic elements of a great thriller.

Think about what makes you jealous. Perhaps someone has more money than you feel they deserve, or they get a job you wanted, or they marry the girl you loved, and so on. How does that make you feel? Write it down. What do you feel like doing about it?

Now magnify it out of all proportion, and apply it to the villain of your story. How jealous is he? (Very!) Is he fully in control of his mind? (Possibly not.) Has he gone totally crazy? (Possibly.) What exactly is he going to do about this situation? (It's going to be bad.)

In real life, you might only dream of doing horrible things to the person you're so jealous of. But when you write thrillers, you can actually do it. It might only be words on paper for now, but who knows, it might end up on the big screen one day!

So, what made you jealous or angry recently, and what did it make you feel like doing in revenge?

27. Lawyers

Some jobs are more likely to put you in contact with villains than others. Police officers and prison staff are obvious ones, but what about the legal profession, especially if they have to make regular court appearances?

Every working day, the lawyer in our story will come into contact (and conflict) with a villain. He might be responsible for sending him to jail.

If the villain's friends and family turn against him, he could find himself in a dangerous position.

And that's just one particular villain on one single day. Our lawyer might be responsible for jailing multiple villains per day, and he might spend a hundred or more days in court each year. The likelihood of someone wanting to exact their revenge for what he did is huge.

Some of these people will be involved in the criminal underworld. They'll have contacts who can do him, and his family, serious damage. Sooner or later, whether he likes it or not, he's going to be involved in his own personal thriller.

What other jobs put you into such close proximity and conflict with known villains? Choose one of these people, make him (or her) the subject of a revenge attack, and write a thriller about it.

28. Misusing the latest technology

It's a good idea to subscribe to as many science and medical news magazines, blogs, and newsletters as you can find – or at least visit their websites regularly. You'll often spot a new discovery or technology that intrigues you and has thriller potential.

As a thriller writer, your immediate thought should always be: how could someone with evil intentions misuse this?

Scour the internet for more information. If the article included references and contacts, use them.

See if you can find connections between this technology and other things. Look for connections that are logical but not too obvious.

[TIP] I find Mind Maps useful for this sort of thing, as you can explore the connections and generate new ideas easily.

Whatever technology it is, if it ever becomes available outside the lab that invented it, someone somewhere will find an immoral use for it. And it's probably one that the inventors never could have envisaged.

The person or people misusing the technology might even be a fellow scientist, or one of their superiors or employers. Or it might be a member of the military or the government. The inventors will probably be dismayed.

Even if the technology never makes it out of the lab, that might not matter either. If anyone gets to hear about it, and they can think of an immoral use for it, they can always break in and steal it.

Right now, most science publications are talking about nanotechnology and quantum computing. They've been talking about this for quite a few years. That means it's probably too late for you. Hundreds of thriller writers, including many well-known ones, will have spotted this, and their novels will be nearing completion. Some have already been published.

So you'll either need to come up with a new angle very quickly, or look for another, perhaps newer technology that isn't being covered widely yet.

It doesn't matter if the technology won't ever develop into anything significant. It can still have plenty of story potential if you can see how it might be abused.

The person who's misusing it might not even have evil intentions; he might just be misguided – as was the case in *Jurassic Park*.

[REVERSAL] Rather than abusing emerging technologies, you could switch this idea around and make the technology the solution to the problem featured in your story. But it might only have worked in the lab so far; it's never been tested in the real world. What happens next should be pretty interesting.

29. Narrow escape

A phrase that often comes to mind when we think of thrillers is "narrow escape." A good example of this is when your hero defuses a bomb, and the timer shows one second remaining until it detonates.

But there are lots of other narrow escapes you can write about. And you can place them throughout the story, not just at the climax. They're a great way of emphasizing how much danger your hero is in.

[EXAMPLE] Let's say your hero is being chased down a narrow alley by some villains in a car. Unable to outrun them, he presses himself against the wall. The car passes by, and although he escapes with his life, his clothes are torn to shreds, and he loses some skin and blood. That was certainly a narrow escape.

See how many other narrow escapes you can think of. You don't have to use all of them in a single story, but it'll be a useful list to keep and refer to in the future when you need ideas. Keep extending your list as you think of more examples.

You could also ask the people you know about any narrow escapes they've had. Most of us have had a few, and they can easily be adapted into dramatic situations for thrillers.

In real life, these situations are often caused by us taking silly risks or losing concentration, or they might just be a complete accident. But in thrillers, a villain will undoubtedly be to blame.

30. News 1

Watch for news stories where things have gone badly wrong. It's even better if the blame can be traced back to one person, or a small but possibly corrupt group.

That might not actually be the case in the real-life story, but it certainly could be in your version of it. Examples might include:

- a rogue trader who causes a bank to collapse
- a successful company suddenly going bust with no warning
- a meltdown at a nuclear power station
- an oil rig blowing up
- a chemical plant leaking toxic gas
- and so on

Using the news story as a reference, write a fictional account of what (might have) happened. Who will you blame in your story? Did he do it deliberately? Or did something distract him or make him lose concentration? Was something in his personal life affecting his ability to make decisions?

What was the sequence of mini-disasters that eventually led to the major disaster? Did he know anything about the mini-disasters? Did he try to do anything about them, or did someone else? Why did that make things worse? What did he do when he realized things were out of control and it was his fault? What happened to the person, the company, and the other employees as a result?

31. News 2

When you watch the news on TV, you'll probably hear about an accident or two. But what if one of them wasn't an accident, it just looked like one? Pick an intriguing real-life accident and use it as the basis for a thriller.

Who is the victim and who is the villain? We'll assume there is a villain, even if there doesn't appear to be one at first sight. Were there any witnesses? If so, does the villain know about them? And will he try to eliminate them, threaten them, bribe them, or something else? How did the villain cause the accident? Why did he do it? Will he get away with it? Has he done this sort of thing before? Was this a one-off or random attack, or part of a series of so-called accidents?

As you think some more about this "accident," see how many questions you can come up with. What really happened, and what alternative explanations can you think of? How could you turn it into a thriller? How could you add a deadline or a ticking clock, and bring the story to a close with a gripping climax? A good way of adding a ticking clock to a story like this might be someone trying to get the victim to the hospital before he dies. But, of course, there are endless obstacles and obstructions in the way. Did the villain put them there, or arrange for someone else to put them there?

Who's next in line for an accident? Let's follow them and see how they get on. And let's also follow the investigator. He's just worked out who the next victim will be, and he's rushing to save him. Will he get there in time? (That's another ticking-clock deadline.) What if he gets held up? Was the hold-up caused by the villain too? Is the investigator about to witness another "accident" that he could have prevented? Or will he find a way of stopping it?

32. Newspapers – financial section

You might not consider the business and financial pages of a newspaper to be particularly thrilling. Like many people, you might even skip them altogether. But they're packed with marvelous ideas for thrillers!

Among all the share prices and exchange rates you'll find tons of intriguing stories:

- brutal company takeovers
- business successes and failures
- bankruptcies
- crooked bosses
- police raids
- insider dealing
- false accounting scandals
- unexpected losses
- firings
- resignations – for all sorts of interesting reasons
- redundancies

- virus and hacker attacks
- and even the occasional kidnapping or assassination

String a few of these together, play "what if," imagine the story playing out in your head in a few different ways – and then write the perfect corporate thriller.

33. Pandemics

There's always a new and ever-more-alarming disease to worry about: HIV/AIDS, bird flu, swine flu, MRSA, vCJD, flesh-eating bugs, and who knows what might be coming next – one dreads to think. But you *should* think, because these diseases (and others like them) can be turned into fantastic thrillers.

There have already been stories about viruses and diseases, of course. That's actually a good thing, because you can use them as a basic template for your own version. But you can make yours a little different by giving it a slight twist or introducing a new angle. For example:

- those who believe it's a punishment from God
- scientists who succumb to the disease themselves
- terrorists and rogue states that immediately add it to their arsenal of weapons
- politicians who try to use it in their favor
- and so on

But don't make your story too different from those that have been written before, especially if they were really successful.

The beginning of your story might follow the typical pattern of the genre: your lead characters examine the victims, try to identify the new disease, and trace its origins and cause. What happens next is up to you – but make sure you refer to the other books and movies in the genre for reference and ideas, and to see how they were structured.

Newspaper archives are a great place to do your research. You should be able to search most of them online, although some have a subscription fee. (Our local library offers this service for free to its members.) See what the newspapers said about the last major disease scare. You'll find plenty of facts, lies, wild speculation and scare-mongering.

Who will suffer the most? Who could benefit from it – politicians, pharmaceutical companies and their stockholders, and so on? Apply your findings to whatever terrible new disease you choose to use (or invent).

34. Paths – difficult

Your hero will have to walk along some difficult paths to get what he wants. The phrase "difficult paths" reminds me of fire-walking, which looks incredibly dangerous, but is actually quite safe if you know the right technique. What other things can you think of that sound more dangerous than they really are?

Think of some other paths (real or metaphorical) that your hero might have to walk over. Let's stick with the fire-walking example and imagine that he has bare feet.

Perhaps his first path in the story is made up of small, rounded pebbles – perfectly safe to walk on, but it might throw him a little off balance from time to time. What sort of situation does this remind you of?

Perhaps it's the everyday work he does. Or his home and family life. Or his relationships.

His next challenge might equate to walking over sharp rocks. It'll hurt a lot more than the pebbles, but he should be safe enough if he takes it slow and steady and doesn't slip or fall too heavily.

His third path might be like walking over broken glass. This time he will almost certainly get hurt and sustain some injuries. He'll probably have considerable doubts about even attempting it. But he should still be able to make it to the other side.

The fourth path will represent his final challenge. This one might be like walking on razor-sharp needles, nails, or blades. It's highly dangerous. It will cause him intense pain. Unless he can find a way of protecting himself, he could be seriously injured – but he might not have time to protect himself. He might lose most of the skin on his feet or even bleed to death before he gets halfway across. Few have been brave (or stupid) enough to attempt it. No one has ever made it all the way across. Until now.

Remember, these aren't actual paths (although they could be). They represent the rising levels of challenge and difficulty your character faces as he progresses through the story. And the increasing risk to his health (and possibly to his life) if things go wrong. And of course things will go wrong, especially when he tries to cross the third and fourth paths.

And if you feel like making things worse for him, you could always set the path on fire.

35. Plans

Most thrillers require the main character to formulate a plan of some kind: an escape plan, a rescue plan, a plan to trap the villain, and so on. There might even be an official plan that states what people should do if a particular event occurs. But in thrillers, things never go according to plan.

So the plan will need to be revised. And then revised again. Urgently. As the situation becomes more and more desperate, the plan will begin to fall apart. Emergency measures will have to be brought in. Unforeseen circumstances will arise that have to be incorporated into the plan.

Eventually, the plan might be discarded. Perhaps it's become irrelevant, or it's holding your hero back – possibly both. He's really under pressure now. From this point on, there are no written instructions to follow, and no guidelines to help him. He's flying by the seat of his pants and making up the plan as he goes along. This will be a real test of how good a hero he is.

36. Plausibility and "truth"

Could the events in your story actually happen? You need to convince your readers that they could. Make them believe in the "truth" of the events – even if they could never really happen, or they're highly unlikely to happen. Make your readers wonder what would happen if such a thing occurred in real life. Make them worry about it. Get them talking about it: the more people they discuss and debate it with, the more books you'll sell.

Imagine that newspapers and magazines publish special features on the "truth" behind your story. Perhaps TV shows will invite experts on to talk about the possibility and probability of such things happening for real, what the consequences would be, and how the world would cope.

There are some great examples:

- *The Da Vinci Code*: kept documentary makers busy for years.
- *Jurassic Park*: could dinosaur DNA really be extracted from the stomach of a mosquito trapped in amber? No, apparently. But it filled newspapers and science magazines for months.
- *Jaws*: the 1974 novel and 1975 movie still make many of us think twice about swimming in the sea.
- *The Silence of the Lambs*: people talked about the book and movie for years afterward.

None of these stories were real, but they were plausible. They had that air of "truth" that's the mark of a great story. And, as we all know, they were all bestsellers, box office smash hits, made their authors a fortune, and they're still remembered and talked about decades later.

37. *Reader's Digest*

You can find the details of a real-life thriller in *Reader's Digest* magazine every month. There are condensed versions of nonfiction books in every issue, and they pack the outline, highlights, climax, and denouement into just a handful of pages. Many of these could be adapted into fiction quite easily.

Examples include accounts from people who have been lost at sea, or on mountains, and so on. Some of them were trapped in burning buildings or in collapsed mines, or they experienced other circumstances where their lives were at risk. Most of them survived, though not always unscathed.

You could also combine incidents from several real-life stories into a single novel, modifying the situations and characters to fit your plot. Or you could try mixing and matching incidents from back issues of the magazine with those from more recent ones.

Pick one incident as the main plot, and then add the others as sub-plots to make an action-packed, thrilling adventure that's full of drama, tension, suspense, and emotion. Some of the incidents should rely heavily on action, while others should center around human-interest issues – and a roller coaster of emotions. If you get this right, you'll create the ultimate thriller.

Reader's Digest is widely available from newsagents and other places that sell magazines, or you can subscribe to it online. Older copies are frequently seen in waiting areas – doctors, dentists, vehicle workshops, and so on.

38. Real life thrills

Where would you go if you wanted to experience a real-life thrill? What excites you like nothing else? A theme park with white-knuckle rides? A horse race or motor race? A boxing match? A stunt show? A circus? Bungee jumping? Paragliding? Sky diving? Swimming with dolphins? Or sharks? Mountaineering? Off-piste skiing? They all allow you to experience thrills on your own terms, in a safe(ish), controlled way. Until things go wrong, that is. Then the thrill can become a thriller.

To be genuinely thrilling, there needs to be an element of risk or actual danger involved. If you go to a properly organized event, there should be minimal danger. But perhaps the event in your story *isn't* properly organized. And even if it is, something might still go wrong – something unforeseen, something criminal, or maybe something evil.

What if someone wants to cause you harm? The easiest way might be to get you while you're taking part in one of these events. A few snips to a safety harness, a few cuts to a rope, a signpost in the wrong place, a hole in the fence ... and you're in serious danger.

Come up with a good reason why the villain wants you harmed, tell the story of what happens, and you've got yourself a great thriller.

39. Research

One thing that particularly stands out when you read a good thriller is that you can tell the writer has done some research.

Whatever the story is about – legal, medical, corporate, police, forensics, armed forces, intelligence, espionage, computers, and so on – the writer has obviously done the job professionally, or gone along and watched someone doing it, interviewed them, taken a tour, attended conferences, read about it extensively, and so on. As a result, he's able to describe each process accurately and in detail. And detail is important in thrillers because lives often depend on it.

Let's say that in your thriller your hero needs to locate and defuse a bomb. You should at least know the basic principles of how to locate, identify and defuse a bomb, even if you couldn't actually do it yourself.

If you want to describe the process in detail in your book, you'll need to speak to a bomb disposal expert, read books and articles and watch videos about how it's done, and read the biographies of people who have done it.

But you don't just want to know about the process – and be able to describe it. You need to know how long it takes, how much training you need, what safety precautions are taken, what it feels like to do it – the first time and subsequently, and so on.

If you're writing a medical thriller, you might need to describe a particular surgical procedure in detail. Readers tend to like this sort of thing. So, again, you'll need to research it, and (if possible) observe the procedure being carried out, either in real life or on video.

You'll also want to learn about the things that can go wrong. Hopefully, the real-life procedure you're observing will go without a hitch. But that needn't be the case in your fictional version.

So, you need to make a research plan. What exactly is your thriller about? What are the crucial details you need to include to make it convincing, realistic and plausible? How can you give your readers an insight into what goes on? How does it affect those involved? How will you find out about these things?

40. Russian roulette

How about adapting a game of Russian roulette into a story? Six chambers in a pistol; five are empty, one contains a bullet. Spin the barrel, pull the trigger, take a chance.

Perhaps in your version, you could have six doors. Behind one lies almost certain death, while the others lead to less dangerous parts of the story.

Or how about if terrorists have planted a bomb under one of six cars in a parking garage? You tell your readers whose cars they are.

They know that one of the lead characters is (probably) about to get blown up. But they don't know which one. Yet.

To build the tension, you might want to string this scene out for a while. The main storyline will follow the main characters as they end their meeting, chat around the water cooler, get into the elevator, arrive in the parking garage, head for the cars, remember something they wanted to say and go back to speak to someone, and finally get into their cars.

At last, we see who gets into the car with the bomb under it. We see the motion sensor rocking and getting ready to trigger…

But you probably won't want to show all of that as one long, uninterrupted sequence. You'll intercut it with other scenes and sub-plots to prolong the suspense even further.

41. Signs of things to come

The first sign of a threat usually comes right at the start of a thriller. But it's often such a tiny little thing that its significance isn't immediately apparent. In fact, it probably goes unnoticed or is shrugged off by the characters as "just one of those things."

- It might be a tiny crack or chip that appears in a sheet of glass.
- It might be a drip from a crack in a pipe.
- It might be a needle on a meter that briefly goes into the red zone before returning to normal.
- It might be a few digits in a column of numbers on a computer screen that are slightly different from the others. Then the screen scrolls up and the anomalous digits disappear. No one notices.

- Someone might suffer a tiny twinge of pain. He winces, shrugs it off, forgets about it, and goes back to whatever he was doing.

- It could be any number of things.

Think about how your thriller begins. What small clues will you give to suggest that something isn't right? It probably won't be enough to worry anyone, but when they look back on it later, or analyze the data, they'll realize that if they'd spotted it in time, and acted upon it, they might have prevented a major disaster.

42. Slow threat

How can something slow be threatening?

Imagine a stream of lava flowing towards a city. It might move really slowly – perhaps just a few feet per day – but it's relentless and unstoppable. If it keeps flowing, the city will be destroyed. There's nothing anyone can do about it. But at least everyone had plenty of time to escape. They might even try digging channels to direct the lava away from the city. But for some reason, they don't work.

What other examples of slow threats can you think of?

It might be a disease that slowly takes over someone's body. It might be years before anyone notices the first symptom. But once they do, it's too late to do anything about it. Is it infectious? How many people are infected? Are we all now in danger?

It might be a plague of animals that slowly but relentlessly expand their territory. And, just to make things worse, they might be poisonous, carry disease, or wipe out the other animals and crops in their path.

To turn this into a thriller, your main character will have to try and stop it. But, as we know, it's unstoppable. It might be slow-moving, and your hero might have plenty of time to prepare for it, or to try several different methods, but success is unlikely. But somehow he'll manage it in the end, against all the odds. (Probably.)

But even if he doesn't succeed, he might at least have paved the way for the next attempt, whenever that might be. Perhaps he could leave a message that will be found in the future. And that might be where your sequel begins...

43. Snatching away victory

Your hero's success often hangs on a single outcome. He's been striving for this one crucial thing throughout the story. If he achieves it, it will make everything right. So, for the last big disaster of your story, just before the climax, you could put it permanently out of his reach.

> [EXAMPLE] Your hero has spent the entire story desperately trying to find the only man in the world who can solve his problem. So you make sure that man dies – maybe just a few minutes before your hero finally reaches him. Your hero might even have been able to save him if he hadn't been delayed by earlier obstacles. But now he's defeated. Everything is lost.
>
> Well, not quite everything. Now he'll have to solve the problem on his own, and prove that *he's* the real hero of the story.

So, who or what is your hero searching for? What is he striving to achieve? How will you make it impossible for him? How will you put the thing he's seeking permanently out of reach?

This is a key moment of crisis in your story. I wouldn't reveal it until at least three-quarters of the way through. Your readers have been following your hero, willing him on, all the way up to this point, and now success has been cruelly snatched from him. This should come as a huge shock to everyone – not just to your hero but to your readers too. Will he give up in despair? He probably thinks about it. But no. He's a hero, so he pushes on. But he has hardly any time left to fix the problem.

44. Spy School

Look out for TV series and documentaries that show how real-life intelligence agents are recruited and trained, and how they operate. This is extremely useful information for thriller writers.

> [EXAMPLE] The best example I've seen was the British TV series *Spy School* (2003) which was hosted by the renegade former intelligence agent David Shayler. It examined how espionage techniques work in the real world, and looked at the work of real-life intelligence agents. It covered surveillance, tailing and bugging, recruitment of agents, torture techniques (and how to resist them), assassinations, codes and code breaking, and more.

45. Story and pace

In a thriller, the story should always come before everything else. Anything that gets in the way just slows it down and irritates your readers. You might love all the well-crafted asides, flashbacks, tangents, sub-sub-plots, and long, poetic descriptions you've included. But they'll have to be removed at editing time.

When you've completed the first draft, put it aside for at least three days (longer if possible) so you get some separation from it. Then read the whole story through from beginning to end, and get some of your most trusted readers to do the same. Everyone should make a note whenever the story diverges from the main plot, or whenever the pace slackens.

If several people agree that a particular scene does this, and it's to the detriment of the story, then it will have to go.

You should be left with a non-stop, fast-moving, tightly focused story that grips your readers from the first page to the last and never lets them go.

You'll need to slow things down occasionally, of course. You need to let your readers and characters catch their breath. For example, your characters could stop running and have an intense discussion from time to time. Or they could reflect on something that's just happened. Or they could pause to formulate a new plan – though they probably get interrupted before it's finalized.

You might need to add these scenes later, at suitable resting points. But make sure they add to the story rather than take away from it. Things might have slowed down for a time, but they're no less compelling and interesting to read. Check with your trusted readers again, and be prepared to make a few more amendments.

46. Stream of consciousness

Here's a technique that works really well when your main character is under severe stress. Take your readers inside his head. Let them see what he's thinking. His words come tumbling out in a confused, overlapping mess. There's no grammar, and little or no punctuation.

It's just broken thoughts, fragments, ideas, interruptions, jokes, panic, terror, thoughts of loved ones left behind, and so on.

> [EXAMPLE] Trapped ... fence, climb it, no time ... hide ... nowhere to hide, got to or he'll get me ... down a manhole ... isn't one ... have to be the fence then ... sitting duck, no choice, got to climb it ... he's coming, run, faster, climb it, jump ...

It accurately conveys your character's thoughts, and the heat and stress of the moment. But it's hard on your readers, so don't keep it up for too long, and don't overuse it.

47. Tension – slowing the pace

A great way of creating tension is to slow the action right down. It also makes a wonderful contrast between scenes, so your story isn't all one big, frenetic rush.

Let's say that you've just described a dramatic car chase through the city and the villain has your hero trapped. You could continue the frenetic pace and have the villain launch an immediate attack. But if you slow things down, and build anticipation and tension, you'll have your readers on the edges of their seats.

Your hero knows he's trapped, and so do your readers. He can hear the villain getting out of his car, cocking his pistol, and stalking towards him. But there's nowhere for him to go. He's going to have to face the villain, one on one. There's a big action scene coming up. But not quite yet ... and we don't know exactly when.

String it out. Keep it nice and slow. The tension is huge, but there's no real action. Let your readers sweat it out along with your hero ... waiting ... waiting.

Describe the villain's every footstep, every crunch on the gravel, every broken twig. We can hear his breathing now. We might even be able to smell him. Your hero knows he's going to be found any second now – there's no doubt about that. He'll just have to wait for the perfect moment and spring into action at the same time that the villain does. Or maybe a fraction of a second before him.

And then the villain is right there. He attacks! Everything returns to full speed, and we're straight into the next full-on action scene.

48. The writer's curse

Have you ever written something fictional and then it actually happened in real life?

It happens to most of us. It's certainly happened to me – several times, in fact – and it can be really annoying. But, by way of compensation, we should be able to get a good story out of it.

What if your main character is writing a crime story? Let's say it's being serialized in a newspaper or magazine as he writes it.

What if the things he writes about start happening? His readers will become very interested in what he has to say. But so will the criminals he writes about. They won't be happy that he seems to know all about their plans. The police will want to know where he's getting his information from. Is he part of the criminal gang? Is he leaking their plans?

His family might disown him, as he seems to be fraternizing with the criminal classes. He must be, because how else could he be privy to that sort of information? His family might even be threatened by the criminals.

But, of course, he doesn't really have access to their plans. He's just writing his crime stories; making it all up. They're coming true, but, as we know, that's what happens when you're a writer. Non-writers might not know that though.

It doesn't have to be a crime story, of course. The author in your story might make up stories about other things that have never happened and are never likely to happen. But they occur shortly after his story is published. Once again, people are going to take a keen interest in him. How can he predict the future with such accuracy? This time, the people paying attention to him might be members of the intelligence services. Perhaps the things he's writing about were meant to be a national secret, known only to the President and a handful of others.

On the other hand, and depending on what sort of event it is, he might be applauded and celebrated for predicting it, or revealing it. But, to make it an interesting story, you can bet that some people won't be happy that he's done it.

> **[NOTE]** The worst thing of all is when the event happens after you've written about it, but before it's been published. People might accuse you of jumping on the bandwagon, being derivative, and lacking imagination.
>
> Even if the writer in your story can prove he wrote it months ago, most people won't be interested. They'll continue to believe their hallucination that he's written about something that has already happened. A writer that can predict the future is too far outside their comfort zone. But they can readily accept that writers write about things that have already happened. So that's what their brains tell them must have happened in this case.

If that happens in your story, what does your writer character do about it? Is there anything he *can* do?

Perhaps he could self-publish his next story, so it gets into print that much sooner. Or he could post it on his blog as he writes it. Or he could send it out to selected readers. That way, if his words come true again, he'll get the kudos (or blame) for predicting it. The big story in the media might then be about *him*: "The incredible story of the man who predicted ... whatever it was."

49. Things you know about

Since you're reading this, there are at least two things you definitely know something about: (a) writing, and (b) the internet. How could you put these two things together to make a thriller?

Perhaps your villain could attack someone or put him in a life-or-death situation by writing something and posting it online.

He might use the internet to find a hacker. He might then pay the hacker to install something on the victim's computer that sends him copies of every email she sends and receives, or the address of every website she visits. He might then pose as one of her friends, or someone she shares a common interest with. He'll be able to gain her confidence, perhaps arrange to meet her in person. But then she finds out he isn't who he claimed to be. She remembers how much she's told him about her life ... and she realizes how much trouble he's in.

You should be able to come up with hundreds of other ideas, based on the topics of writing and the internet. They could of course be separate topics: thrillers about writers, and thrillers based on the internet. Or you could combine them.

But I'm sure you know about a lot more things than just writing and the internet. You probably know plenty of things about your job, the people you work with, your family, neighbors, activities, vacations, hobbies, and so on. It's worth making a list of the things you know about.

And then you could think about all the people you know and what they might know about.

The villain in your story will know other people too. Some of the things they know might be extremely useful to him. So, what might his friends and business associates know about ? How could he use those things to cause other people problems, and perhaps put their lives in danger?

Once you've come up with an idea – perhaps based on something one of your friends or colleagues knows about – you have the starting point for your thriller.

50. Thirty-year rule

Things often need to kept secret for reasons of national security. In the UK, the Thirty-Year Rule says that some of these things can be made public after 30 years. (Other countries have similar rules, but the time period might differ.) It's always worth looking out for items released under these laws when they appear in the news. You might even be able to find a website or government document that lists the items as they're released.

Big-name writers and publishers will immediately pounce on the major items, of course. But there will undoubtedly be plenty of smaller, less sensational items that they overlook or don't have the time to deal with. You should be able to turn one or more of these into a fantastic thriller.

You can base your story on the real-life incident, or make up one that's inspired by the document you saw.

51. Thriller formula

Here at ideas4writers, we love formulas. Here's a good one for writing thrillers, courtesy of John Baldwin:

- The hero is an expert.
- The villain is an expert.
- You must watch all of the villainy over the villain's shoulder.
- The hero has a team of experts in various fields behind him.
- Two or more on the team must fall in love.
- Two or more on the team must die.
- The villain must turn his attention from his initial goal to the team.
- The villain and the hero must live to do battle again in the sequel.
- All deaths must proceed from the individual to the group. For example, never say "The bomb exploded and 700 people were killed." Start with something like: "Stan and Martha were walking in the park with their granddaughter when the earth opened up."
- If you get bogged down, just kill somebody.

52. Thrillers the easy way

Thrillers are one of the biggest-selling categories of fiction, but they can be notoriously difficult to write.

Here are some easy ways to get started:

Look at some of the stories you've written in the past, even if they weren't thrillers. Could you introduce a life-or-death situation? Could you make the characters fight to save each other against a time limit? Could you add significantly more twists, turns, obstacles, and surprises? Could you raise the stakes, so that the thing they're either fighting to get, or fighting to stop, matters more?

Another way is to take a story from another genre and keep raising the stakes. Most storylines from other genres can be turned into thrillers just by doing this. Raise the stakes, add more complications, and increase the tension and suspense. You might then end up with a comedy thriller, a crime thriller, a historical thriller, a romantic thriller, a psychological thriller, and so on.

> [TIP] Don't forget to check out our other collections of ideas in other genres. You should be able to adapt most of them into thrillers.
>
> Our thriller storyline ideas are coming up shortly too, starting from idea #62.

53. Trapped together

What if your hero sets a trap for the villain, but gets trapped in it himself? And what if the trap also works a second time, and traps the villain, as originally intended? Now your hero and villain are trapped together. They might fight initially, but eventually they'll realize that the only way they're getting out is if they work together.

Will they co-operate? Or are they stuck there until someone rescues them? What will happen afterward? Will they continue their feud as if nothing had happened? Or has something changed between them? They might have had a long talk while they were trapped. Will they now see each other in a different light? Will they be friends? Perhaps they'll even work together. How will this affect what has happened in the story up to that point? How will it change the climax and outcome?

For example, the villain might reveal information about the leaders of the gang he belongs to. The gang won't be happy when they find out about this, of course. So now your thriller has an interesting extra angle.

54. Trust, suspicion, and doubt

Suspicion and doubt can be significant factors in thrillers. Imagine, for example, that you have to place your life in the hands of a stranger, but you have no idea which side he's on.

Trust is another important factor. You might remember the slogan from *The X-Files* TV series: "Trust no one." So our hero trusts no one, suspects everyone, and doubts everything. As a result, his life is going to be pretty tense – which is just as it should be in a good thriller.

But there will come a time when he'll have to trust someone, or believe something, or stop doubting for a few moments. And that might be his biggest mistake ... with potentially fatal consequences.

55. Viewpoint – switching

Try writing one chapter from the good guys' point of view, and the next one from the bad guys' perspective, and keep alternating between them throughout the story until you reach the climax.

Your readers will then know what each side is planning, but the characters themselves will not. This puts your readers in a superior position and enhances their sense of anticipation. They can't wait to see whether your hero will fall into the trap that the villain has laid for him. And that, of course, means they'll keep reading.

56. Villain – deliberate

The villain in this story deliberately sets out to cause trouble. But what sort of harm does he intend causing, and why? Here are some examples.

- Power: to put himself in a high-ranking position so he can feel superior or have control over other people's lives.

- Sex: for some people, the urge to have sex is more than they can resist, even if they have to break the law to get it.

- Money: some people have a compulsion to acquire as much money as possible; others have a compulsion to spend as much as possible. Either way, they'll need a lot of it, and they'll do whatever it takes to get it.

- Addiction: if he's a drug addict, he'll need money to buy more drugs; his craving for drugs will take priority over any concerns or feelings for anyone else. He might even steal from his own family.

- Mental illness: he might hear voices in his head telling him to commit certain acts.

- Jealousy or envy: he wants what someone else has, or he wants something that's better than theirs, and he can't control that urge.

- Competition: he might try to outdo other villains. An example of this actually happened in the real world: two rival groups of computer hackers released viruses. They kept refining them and releasing new versions in an attempt to infect more computers than their rivals.

- Brainwashing: he might belong to a cult or extremist religious group, and they might have brainwashed him. He might now believe that what he's doing is right. They might even have promised him a reward – though they may have been lying about that.

Other reasons might include:

- Revenge.

- Ethnic cleansing.

- Following in his father's footsteps.

- And many more.

We're barely scraping the surface here. A few minutes spent exploring each of these examples in more detail, or extending the list, should generate plenty of great ideas for thrillers.

> **[EXTENSION]** There are several books available that look at the psychology of the criminal mind. These make fascinating and inspiring reading for crime, horror, mystery and thriller writers.

57. Villain – nervous

What type of villain is likely to worry your hero the most? A nervous one!

A nervous villain is probably inexperienced, insecure, and not following a clear, well-thought-out plan. He'll act rashly, on the spur of the moment. He could panic at any time, lose control of the situation, and just start shooting. Innocent people could get hurt.

A more experienced villain won't be so nervous, and he'll remain in control. That makes the situation much safer: he'll only shoot if he means to. But you still wouldn't want to spring any surprises on him.

It's easy enough to tell when a villain is nervous:

- stuttering
- sweating
- fumbling
- shaking
- dropping things
- long periods of thinking
- he keeps checking the time
- he keeps checking his phone, waiting for backup or further instructions
- he keeps checking the windows
- he bites his nails

- he won't talk – or he won't shut up
- he fires his gun by accident
- he has flashes of bad temper and swearing
- he makes rash decisions that make no sense
- he frequently changes his mind
- and so on

The best we can hope for is that the incident comes to an end quickly and safely. And the best way of doing that is for your hero to take control of the situation himself.

58. Villain – trusted friend

What if one of your hero's most trusted friends turned out to be the villain? But let's say your hero doesn't discover this until the climax of the story.

They might have depended on each other to get this far. Perhaps they've saved each other's lives more than once. Surely there's an unbreakable bond between them now? No. As soon as they find what they were looking for, the so-called friend pulls his gun on your hero. He doesn't need his help any more; he wants it all for himself.

How will your hero get out of this? Well, he'll obviously find a way. Heroes are highly resourceful!

But let's think about his so-called friend who has turned out to be the villain. You'll need to let your readers know there's something not quite right with this guy. Some readers won't notice these hints, and those who do might think they're insignificant. But, just like a good mystery story, nothing in a thriller should ever be insignificant. On a second reading, your readers will notice that the clues were there all along:

- He hangs up the phone without comment when your hero walks into the room.
- He refuses to answer some of your hero's questions, or gives an answer that doesn't make sense, or sounds like a lie.
- We see him talking to someone who's hidden in the shadows, and we can't quite tell who it is.
- He rushes to collect the morning mail and hides one of the letters.
- Someone proves he's a liar. For example, another character says she saw him at a particular location, but he'd already told your hero he wasn't there.
- He always checks to make sure no one can see him or overhear him.
- And so on.

You should be able to come up with plenty more of these.

Incidentally, the best places to plant all of these subtle clues are in the busy action scenes. Things are happening quickly, and your readers are completely caught up in it all. They might not notice (or remember) a tiny detail if it doesn't seem to matter right now.

Another good place is right at the beginning of the story when we're still getting to know the characters.

59. War

Wartime always brings out the best and worst in people. And there are plenty of wars to choose from if you want to use a real one as the basis for your thriller, including historic battles, the two world wars, and modern conflicts.

Much of what went on then (or is still going on) is shrouded in secrecy. That's good news for thriller writers because you can make up plausible-sounding incidents and no one can question whether they actually happened. You can send your hero on a fictional mission whose outcome might change the entire course of the war – and therefore world history.

We all know how the wars of the past ended, of course, but we don't know about the vital (but highly secretive) role your hero played in them – or how differently things might have turned out if he'd failed.

60. Weaknesses and different thinking

Many thrillers begin with a weakness of some kind. Often, it's the villain's weakness – although we might not realize he's the villain yet. He might actually seem quite normal, with no criminal history, and no evil intentions. He might think he's doing the right thing.

For example, someone might have good intentions but fail to think through the consequences of their actions. So in this case he suffers from a weakness of logic.

Let's imagine that a farmer is upset that pests are ruining crops. He sprays his land with an unapproved pesticide, without waiting for permission from the authorities. Unfortunately, there's a serious problem with the pesticide, and there's a good reason why it hasn't been approved. When it ends up in the city's water supply, we have a thriller on our hands: the authorities have to race to stop it from killing everyone. So an honest and decent citizen – the farmer who thought he was protecting his livelihood – has unwittingly, become the "villain" because he didn't think through what might happen.

Or you could have a weakness of willpower. A security guard is hired to protect something valuable but he's overcome by the desire to have it for himself. He switches from being a friendly, co-operative member of the public to a ferocious "villain" who will stop at nothing to get what he wants.

Another example might be someone who realizes that a new invention could have military uses. But the inventor intended it to benefit mankind. The "villain" in this case might not be evil, and he might believe he's doing the right thing: the invention will help defend the country he loves. But the inventor doesn't want his work to be used as a weapon, and he tries to stop him. Conflict is inevitable, and if you keep escalating it, you could end up with an incredible thriller.

In fact, it might be hard to determine exactly who the villain is in a story like this. And that will make things *really* interesting. You could even mess with your readers by getting them to think that first one, then the other is the villain. Switch between them repeatedly. Only at the climax will you reveal which one is the hero and which one is the villain. Up until that point, it could go either way. Which one will it be?

What other situations like this can you think of, where a person initiates a thriller because of a weakness, thoughtless action, uncontrollable urge, or a different way of thinking, having previously led a blameless life?

61. Worse and twist

Sometimes, when everything seems hopeless for your hero, you need to find a way of getting him out of trouble. An interesting way of doing this is to have things suddenly get even worse, but then twist it to give him the upper hand.

[EXAMPLES]

The villain stabs him, injuring him badly but not killing him. Your hero now has the knife.

The villain hits your hero over the head with his gun after running out of bullets, injuring him but not fatally. The villain has no further use for the gun, and he leaves it at the scene. Your hero now has the gun. And earlier in the story you showed him stopping to pick up some of the bullets that the villain dropped.

Someone who's been battling for a promotion learns that his bitter rival has been given the job – and his first task is to fire your hero. Your hero has been finally released from a binding contract that was preventing him from taking the job he really wanted.

Part 2: Storylines

62. Storyline: 9/11 part two: Anarchy in the UK

It's like 11th September 2001 all over again – but possibly worse – and this time the targets are all in the UK. Once again, terrorists use planes to attack important buildings and landmarks: Buckingham Palace, the Houses of Parliament, the London Stock Exchange, and so on. The Prime Minister are leading members of the royal family are killed, along with hundreds or thousands of others.

The planes involved have just taken off from Heathrow or Gatwick Airports (perhaps both), and are full of passengers and fuel. They're hijacked and diverted into central London, where they crash in massive fireballs. The whole thing is over within a few minutes. There was no warning and no time for the authorities to react.

How did the terrorists get weapons onto the planes? Perhaps they had agents working as aircraft engineers or as part of the ground crew or cabin crew. Somehow they all passed the vetting procedures. (Journalists have bypassed security several times.) They may have stashed weapons on the relevant planes.

Let's say that the usual terrorist organizations claim responsibility – most notably al-Qaeda or ISIL. But who can Britain attack in revenge? The obvious targets – Afghanistan, Iraq, Syria – have already been dealt with. Or have they?

As the terrorists continue to act, perhaps more needs to be done to wipe them out. The war on terror will have to be expanded.

Which countries will take Britain's side and join the fight? Which ones will say Britain brought it on itself and refuse to take part? And which countries will side with the terrorists and supply them with arms and aid?

63. Storyline: bad to worse

Some victims suffer increasingly severe attacks. At first, they might only be mild beatings – hardly worth complaining to the police about, assuming they know who did it and why. But then things get worse: a broken limb or two. And it could get much worse than that next time.

Why is this happening? Do they owe the villains money? Have they entered into some sort of agreement that they can't now fulfill?

Things continue to get worse. Perhaps one or more of their digits or limbs are cut off; perhaps they're raped; maybe they're shot or stabbed but not fatally ... yet.

They fear for their lives now, and some of them seek protection. Some go to the police, others hire bodyguards. But they all get killed.

Or perhaps we might let one of them survive – just for a little while. Perhaps he can reveal what went on and identify the villain(s). Does he live long enough to see them convicted, sent to prison, or executed? That's up to you.

While he's alive, though, he reveals a desperate tale of horror and suspense. You could tell the whole story in flashback, starting with his dramatic escape from the villain's clutches. He can then tell us what happened, before finally expiring, or being wheeled off for surgery, or being taken away by a nurse because he's exhausted.

But who is he telling the story to?

64. Storyline: bad wife

A man should always choose his wife wisely. But this one didn't, and now he's paying the price.

After a few years of apparently blissful marriage, his wife starts having affairs. That's not, in itself, the end of the world. The real problems begin when she leaves one of her lovers for another. And then she leaves that one for yet another. Unfortunately, these men were not the best choices – as her husband is about to find out. Their desire for revenge, and their cruel ability to carry it out, astonish him.

Let's say that she has a relationship with the doctor that was caring for their sick daughter. When she ends that relationship, the doctor gives their daughter an overdose and kills her – or very nearly kills her.

She might have ended the relationship with the doctor because she'd started having an affair with the builder who was renovating their house. When she ends that relationship too, the builder abandons the job and takes away the props that were holding the house up. It collapses during the night.

Of course, if she's left the builder, that probably means she's found herself yet another lover. Who could it be this time, and what damage will he cause when she ends the relationship? Her husband, now homeless, broke and almost mad with grief, struggles to find out.

And then he has a supreme battle on his hands as he tries to stop his wife's latest spurned lover from inflicting the worst damage of all. Whatever that might be…

65. Storyline: cave hostages

The owner of a large and impressive cave system encourages people to visit it. He particularly welcomes visits from schools. But things go seriously wrong when the entrance collapses while a large group of children from a private school is inside. The children all have wealthy parents, and it soon becomes apparent that the owner of the caves caused the collapse himself.

Now that he has them trapped, he posts armed guards at the entrance to turn rescuers away. In the event of an attack, the guards have been instructed to detonate bombs that will cause the entire cave system to collapse. The owner demands a massive ransom before anyone will be allowed in or out.

Because of the urgency of the situation – no food or water, a limited supply of air, and the kids are in the dark – the police advise the parents to pay the ransom. They will try to get the money back later. However, many of the parents, although wealthy, can't get their hands on that sort of money at short notice – it's tied up in assets. Many of those who are able to pay are concerned that the police will screw things up, and not only will they lose their money but their children too.

With time running out, two factions form. The first group, led by the police, try to raise the ransom money and negotiate with the cave owner to let rescuers in. The second group employs their own advisers, security crew and engineers and starts digging a second entrance into the cave, keeping it a secret from the guards and owner. But they're jeopardizing the safety of all the children if their plan is discovered. What will happen?

66. Storyline: crash!

There's an enormous car crash, with dozens of vehicles involved. In the tangle of wreckage, some people are already dead, some are near death, and others will survive if they get to the hospital within the "golden hour." Tell the story of several of these individuals.

Pick the most interesting ones and get your readers closely involved with them before the accident occurs. Make them care and worry about what will happen to them. Some of them will live, and some will die.

You could include details of harrowing rescue attempts, and show how the emergency services struggle to carry out their duties.

Perhaps the emergency services have trouble even reaching the scene. Commuters are stuck in long tailbacks, and they're angry. What do a few dead people matter when they have meetings to attend and children to get to school on time? They're trying to push through, and they're blocking things up even worse.

Meanwhile, some of the emergency personnel are cutting people out of cars and starting the rescue. But they have their own demons and personal issues to cope with. Flashbacks and nightmares slow them down or spoil their concentration.

One (or more) of the vehicles that crashed might be involved in a crime – perhaps a kidnapping, or someone making a getaway from a robbery. Or they might be smuggling drugs or weapons. Items in the car might need to be hidden or gotten rid of. The villains might be armed and extremely agitated. They'll need to be disarmed (perhaps by shooting them) so that the other victims can be rescued safely.

Meanwhile, time is running out, and the end of the golden hour is approaching. Some people that we think will survive won't make it. Others that we think have no chance might somehow pull through.

Once they get to the hospital, surgeons battle to save them. Hospital resources are suddenly overwhelmed. Someone with a minor injury sees people being wheeled straight into the operating theater. He's been waiting for hours already, and now it looks as if he could be here all night. How dare these people jump the queue! He might injure himself more seriously in an attempt to get treatment sooner.

The timeline of your story might cover no more than a couple of hours. Or you could spread it over 24 or 48 hours.

You could also include an epilogue that lists all the characters and gives a brief summary of what happened to them.

67. Storyline: crooked lawyers

It's often said that the only winners in legal cases are the lawyers. But what if the lawyers were deliberately extending or delaying cases unnecessarily? They might present ridiculous evidence and make false claims against the other party, or blow up the smallest issue into a major drama, simply to make more money from their clients. They don't care whether they win the case or not; the longer they can drag it out, the more money they'll make.

What if the prosecuting and defending lawyers are in cahoots – particularly if both sets of clients are wealthy and can afford a lengthy legal battle? Their clients might demand a swift end to the case – and their lawyers might constantly reassure them that this is exactly what they're getting. But, of course, they aren't. There's always another delay, and yet more legal work that needs doing to resolve it.

A third legal team might then be called in to investigate one or both of the original teams, accusing them of spinning out the case.

Where will it all end? Who will win in this case, and who will lose? What sort of bribery, corruption, scandals and false accounting will be uncovered? Who threatens whom? Who sleeps with whom?

This is a chance to devise an elaborate plot that will intrigue your readers. See if you can end the story with an unforgettable climax that has them on the edges of their seats. Perhaps something happens with just moments to spare: maybe someone runs into the courtroom with a new piece of evidence just as the judge is about to deliver his verdict.

On the other hand, that new piece of evidence might just prove that the preceding months or years of the case were a complete waste of time – and money. They might have to go back to the beginning and start all over again. Perhaps with a fresh set of lawyers.

68. Storyline: Death Row

Those who have been sentenced to death often remain on Death Row for years. There are all sorts of procedures to go through, appeals to be heard, new evidence to be considered, appeals for clemency, and so on. It all takes time.

Let's imagine that a convicted killer has come close to being executed several times, but something has always happened at the last minute to halt it. While news of yet another stay of execution might come as a relief, it's no kind of life either. Sometimes he wishes they'd go ahead and kill him so it'll all be over. He can't remember how many last meals he's had.

Then one day he thinks he's finally reached the end. He's strapped to a table in the execution chamber, the drugs are injected, he's unconscious, his thoughts fade, and he's at peace ... ah, blessed release; it's all over.

But he wakes up in his cell again: apparently there was another last-second reprieve. He's furious. His demands that they kill him are ignored. His demands that they give him the drugs and materials so that he can kill himself are refused.

How long can this go on for? What will happen? Will he be released? Did he actually commit the crime? Will the victim's family join his own family's campaign for his release? Or will he finally be killed?

Perhaps he's there for so long that he eventually dies of old age or disease. What will the victim's family think if that happens? Will they be pleased? Or furious that he wasn't sufficiently punished?

> [EXTENSION] Somehow, our Death Row prisoner is now a free man. Perhaps he escaped, or perhaps he was released. Either way, he resolves to help other people on Death Row.
>
> He sets up a secret organization that puts an insider in the prison, perhaps working as a guard. He smuggles in drugs, guns, knives, tranquilizer darts, and so on. Prisoners who want to escape now have the means to do so. Those who want to kill themselves also have the means to do so. In a matter of days, Death Row is empty. So now what?
>
> Well, there are other Death Rows in other states. He could continue his mission there – unless someone can stop him. The prisoners and the criminal fraternity are firmly on his side. The prisons might

impose a ban on recruiting new guards, but that can only last for so long. There are ways around the new and improved vetting procedures. And there's always the possibility that they can corrupt an existing guard anyway: perhaps one who has nothing to lose.

69. Storyline: deranged patient?

The woman seemed pleasant enough the first time the doctor saw her. Perhaps she had a respiratory infection that wouldn't clear up. He gave her a prescription and she left. A week or two later she was back again, glowing with health but complaining of something more personal. "Wouldn't you rather see a female doctor?" he asks. "No," she says; she would much rather see him. He carries out an intimate inspection at her request but finds nothing wrong – though he notes that she seemed to enjoy it. "There's nothing wrong with you," he assures her. And she leaves.

But she soon comes back, wanting him to check her again. "Something doesn't feel quite right," she tells him. Again, he checks her but finds nothing wrong.

Her visits become more regular after this. She begins asking him about his private life, and her questions gradually became more personal.

He refers her to a hospital consultant, but when she comes back again, he can tell from her records that she didn't go.

Then she changes her job. Perhaps she becomes a receptionist at his surgery, or a cleaner for his wife or neighbor, or a nanny for his children. She moves house so she can live near him.

He arrives home one day and finds her sitting on his couch. His wife has left him a note. It says: "She's told me everything that's been going on between you. I've taken the children, and I'm not coming back."

She sits there smiling at him. "Can I cook you something, darling?" she asks.

Where will the story go from there? Is she as deranged as she seems? How much danger is the doctor in? Will she say "If I can't have you then no one can" and try to kill him?

The only thing that's certain at this point is that it won't end the way she hopes it will.

70. Storyline: drug trial

A medical research company recruits volunteers to test their new drugs. Many of the volunteers are students. In this particular trial, they're given a drug that is supposed to thin their blood. Although it worked well on animals, there seems to be no response in the human volunteers, which takes the researchers by surprise. They increase the size of the doses, but still nothing happens.

But what they haven't realized is that the drug is being stored in the volunteers' fatty tissues. Once it reaches saturation point – and especially if the volunteer exercises vigorously or is hungry, and his body starts digging into its fat reserves – the drug is released into his bloodstream in a massive dose. Their red blood cells and bone marrow are destroyed, and their blood becomes a pale-pink watery fluid that can't hold oxygen. The volunteers fall unconscious and die within minutes.

Unfortunately, this all happens after the researchers have stopped monitoring the volunteers. As the drug seemed to have no effect on humans, they'd abandoned the trial. Most of the volunteers have been sent home. The last few might still be being monitored by nurses, but as they're all lying down and are well fed, they show no symptoms.

In your story, you could follow some of the volunteers as they start to become seriously ill. Some of them might try (but fail) to save the others, before succumbing themselves. They might call the research center for help, but the only people on duty are the nurses, and they don't know what to do. Perhaps they try to contact the researchers, but they can't be reached. And even if they could be reached, what could they actually do?

You could also follow some of the volunteers before the trial begins, so your readers get to know them and develop an emotional bond. You could show them needing the money for their families, spotting the advertisement, and signing up for the trial.

By the time the nurses manage to track down the researchers, many of the volunteers are already dead. The survivors are given repeated blood transfusions, but the drug remains in their tissues and continues to destroy their blood. They can't make any new blood for themselves because their bone marrow has been destroyed. So they'll need continuous blood transfusions just to keep them alive, followed by bone marrow transplants.

Although the volunteers signed a standard disclaimer when they agreed to take part, they were also told the drugs would have a minimal effect on them, their health would never be in any danger, and their blood would return to normal afterward. They should never have been given such massive doses, even if the drug seemed to be having no effect. The survivors, and the relatives of those who died, therefore decide to take legal action against the research company. And that could add yet another layer to an already-fascinating thriller.

74. Storyline: DUI

A group of hoodlums, high on drink and drugs, hold a car race along a stretch of road – the M25 orbital motorway around London would be good for this. Finishing first, or getting the fastest time, and getting a "buzz" is all that matters. They don't care who they hit or kill along the way – they won't be stopping until they cross the finish line.

Some of the cars might have been stolen. Their owners (or their children) might be forced to sit in the back, not knowing if they'll come out of this alive.

One (or more) of the racers might deliberately cause a fatal crash to block the road and stop those behind him from passing him or beating his time. Perhaps the other racers force their way past (or through) the blockage anyway, maybe killing or injuring more people in the process.

The police or military might be authorized to use lethal force to stop them. But there could be innocent victims in the backs of some of the vehicles. Do the authorities know that?

75. Storyline: execution witness

This story is about an ordinary man who has a compulsion to witness an execution. He's obsessed with the idea. It's all he can think about. Perhaps a friend or relative has witnessed one and told him about the experience, and now he needs to see one for himself.

He applies to be a witness to an execution in all of the American states that have capital punishment, but nothing ever comes of it. He contacts other countries to ask if he can be a witness there, but they all refuse. In the end, he realizes that there are only two options: he must either become a victim himself – perhaps by surviving an attack by a serial killer, or he must be a close family member of a victim. The killer also needs to be caught and sentenced to death – and even then he might be held on Death Row for a decade or more. That's no good to the guy in our story. He needs to find somewhere where executions are carried out soon after the death sentence is passed. And that means going to another, more dangerous, country.

He doesn't want to be the victim himself, of course. Perhaps he selects family members he doesn't like and arranges for them to go abroad. Perhaps he takes them on vacation. Then he puts them in dangerous situations in the hope that they'll be attacked. He also needs to make sure the villain is identified and caught.

Naturally, when several members of the same family become victims of separate, seemingly random attacks, the police become suspicious. They're even more suspicious when a video recording of each attack arrives in the mail the following day.

Eventually, the police work out what's going on and who's behind it all. Using information supplied by the family, they deduce who the next victim will be and when the attack is likely to occur. But they don't have much time, and it might already be too late.

The hero of your story might be the police detective who pieces all the facts together and is able to identify the villain (i.e. the guy who wants to witness the execution) and his mad obsession. The detective might have an obsessive compulsion himself – his determination to always find the truth.

You might like to consider giving the story an ironic ending where the guy who wanted to witness an execution ends up getting executed himself. (Or would that be too predictable? Perhaps you can think of a better twist.)

73. Storyline: false evidence

A man hires a private detective to help him find out who killed his wife – but he actually killed her himself.

He hopes the detective will find evidence to prove (or at least suggest) that someone else is the killer. The police undoubtedly have their suspicions about him, but they don't have any conclusive proof yet.

The detective gives the man regular progress reports, letting him know what he's found so far, and what specific thing he'll be looking for next. But whenever he does this, the exact piece of evidence he needs always turns up, usually within just a few hours. It all seems too easy – and highly suspicious. (The man is, of course, planting the evidence himself.)

At their next meeting, the detective mentions a rather bizarre piece of evidence that he needs to find. Our man will need to go to great lengths to acquire this thing and plant it where it will be discovered. And that gives the detective the opportunity to follow him. Sure enough, he catches him in the act and confronts him. The man kills the detective out of desperation.

A few days later, the police break into the detective's office, as he's been reported missing. They learn from his records that he was trying to find the person who killed the man's wife. Our man is now the key suspect in two murders.

He continues to plant false evidence that proves he didn't kill his wife. But he now also has to devise and plant a trail of evidence which shows he didn't kill the detective. He decides to make all the evidence point to someone else. But who? Could he make it look as if the detective killed his wife? Will he hire another detective? Will he end up having to kill him too?

Things have moved up another level now, and they could turn very nasty indeed. And they were pretty nasty to start with.

74. Storyline: French nuclear war

France is at war. You can decide who they're at war with, but it's not Britain (for reasons which will become obvious in a moment).

The war has escalated, and the country France is at war with (plus its allies) decide to drop a nuclear bomb on Paris, or another part of northern France. However, the bomb they're planning to use is so powerful that it will also destroy part of southern England.

The allies are determined to drop the bomb, but Britain (which has now become one of the allies fighting against France) vigorously opposes it. As the debate rages on, and the date on which the bomb will be dropped grows ever closer, Britain's armed forces and intelligence services work frantically behind the scenes trying to persuade France to surrender.

When that fails, and a nuclear attack looks imminent, the British Government needs to consider swapping sides and joining France to fight against the allies and prevent the bomb from being dropped. That's a huge risk, because British cities might then be targeted directly. But perhaps Britain and France could bomb the allies first.

75. Storyline: hacked

In this story, a group is campaigning against a particular cause, and they start attacking and defacing websites which support it. How do they gain access to those sites? They'll need to recruit hackers. Where do they find them? How do they persuade them to join their organization? The so-called "dark web" might be a good place to start – if they can figure out how to access it.

What else might they do to damage the organizations which support the cause? They could send out millions of spam emails in the organization's name, in the hope that they get kicked offline or have to pay a hefty fine. They could spread malicious rumors online. They could stage protests outside their buildings. They could send protest letters and petitions to the government.

When they deface the websites, will they make it obvious? Or will they covertly change links, add viruses, or add spurious files or copyrighted information in the hope that the organization gets sued?

There are plenty of other things that might happen. And presumably someone stops them in the end. But how? You should find plenty of ideas if you dig through the technology news stories of the past few years.

76. Storyline: heart-stopping

When you think of thrillers, one of the phrases that might come to mind is "heart-stopping." And that instantly gives me an idea for a story...

Let's say that some people have been kidnapped – it's up to you to decide who they are. The kidnappers demand a ransom, but the payment is refused. They could start shooting the hostages, but that's not nearly cruel enough for them. And anyway, they've got a stolen bottle of potassium chloride. The hostages are strapped down and given injections of the drug. Their hearts stop. The villains set fire to the building and leave.

A particularly interesting aspect of this case is that the villains knew precisely what they were doing. The dose they gave each hostage was carefully calculated. How did they know what the dosages should be? They must have had medical training.

Let's say that one or two of the victims survive and their hearts start beating again. Who miscalculated their dosages – or was it deliberate? The survivors now have to try to free themselves, free the others, and restart everyone's hearts before the fire reaches them, and while escape is still possible.

It's unlikely that they'll be able to save everyone. Even if they do, some probably won't survive. They need to focus on those with the best chances of making it. And that will undoubtedly mean leaving behind someone they're close to.

I don't see this idea as a story in itself, but it would make a fantastic major scene or climax in a novel or screenplay.

77. Storyline: hypnotic religion

A TV hypnotist/illusionist decides to use his powers to start a new "religion." He can easily convince people that he has mystical powers, and he promises them that if they join him, they too will be able to perform these miracles. Once he has established a large enough following, they can all work together to solve the world's problems and enter a new age of enlightenment. All he asks for in return is a large sum of money – to "prove their faith."

As new members sign up, he whisks them away to a month-long retreat where he repeatedly hypnotizes them. While they're in a trance, he instructs them on how to perform the illusions. When they wake up they don't remember the trickery; they just know that they can now perform the same "miracles." They go out into the world demonstrating their powers and recruiting others.

Naturally, things get out of hand. The police investigate the hypnotist (known to his followers as the "Mighty Leader" or something along those lines) and keep him under constant surveillance. What will he do with the huge amount of money his followers have "donated"? Will he use it to do good deeds? Will he spend it on a luxury lifestyle for himself and his family? Or will he put it to a more sinister use?

Let's also say that a senior police officer has joined his "religion." And as far as he's concerned, it's all genuine and legitimate. Not only is there nothing to investigate, he also wants his colleagues to join.

Increasing numbers of people now want to join, but many of them don't have enough money to pay the "fee of faith" required to get in. Some of them turn to crime to get it.

Let's send someone in undercover to try to find out what's really going on. Perhaps he pretends to be in a trance during the hypnosis sessions so he can learn the truth behind the "miracles." But can he resist the Mighty Leader's hypnotic powers? And what will happen if the Mighty Leader discovers who he is and why he's really there? The situation could (and probably will) become dangerous. And that could lead to a dramatic and thrilling rescue scene at the climax.

78. Storyline: invalid evidence

Law enforcement agencies panic when criminals adopt new tactics that render most of their evidence invalid. Blood is being stolen from blood banks and left at crime scenes. As a result, anyone who has donated blood recently can't be prosecuted. There's a rush of new blood donors – but who are the genuine donors and who has evil intentions? Is there any way of telling them apart?

Fingerprints are next on the criminals' list. They might start accidentally-on-purpose dropping things, asking other people to kindly pick them up, and then leaving them at crime scenes. The criminals themselves all wear gloves of course, or cover their fingerprints with liquid skin or glue, or file them off. This practice spreads throughout the criminal classes, and as a result, all of the fingerprints found at crime scenes become useless.

Gradually, the criminals work their way through the entire range of forensic techniques the agencies have at their disposal. Somehow, they devise ways of bypassing them, screwing them up, or rendering them inadmissible in court. What will happen next?

79. Storyline: kidnapped and killed

Kidnapping is one of the most intense ordeals a person can experience. These days, the kidnappers might also be terrorists with impossible demands – and they're more than willing to kill their victims.

Imagine that one of the main characters in your story has been kidnapped. The kidnappers have imposed a time limit, but since no one will agree to their demands, it's more like a countdown to death as far as the victim is concerned.

But, since he has nothing to lose, he's willing to take crazy risks. If he dies in the process, well, they were going to kill him anyway, so what does it matter? At least he'll have tried. And the people who matter to him might get to hear that he tried – and that's important to him.

Let's say that he somehow manages to escape. He sends a message to his rescuers, who we've seen working frantically in the background, their efforts constantly hindered by a seemingly indifferent government. But the kidnappers catch him and shoot or stab him before the rescuers can reach him. They leave him for dead ... but he isn't quite dead. Somehow he survives, and he eventually makes it home – with enough adventure stories to last a lifetime.

But he's a man of action. He's not going to sit around telling stories forever. He knows how the kidnappers operate. He knows their methods, their personnel, and their hiding places. So when someone else gets kidnapped, he books himself onto the first plane there, ready to offer his services.

Will the terrorists remember him? Will they think they've seen a ghost? Will they try to kill him again? Will they make sure of it this time? Or will he escape serious injury and fight on ... and perhaps continue to do so in several sequels too?

80. Storyline: kidnapped killer

Our hero finds a young woman crying in the street and invites her into his house for a cup of tea. She is reluctant, but he insists, and eventually she agrees. She won't stop crying though.

But then she reveals her problem. She has been kidnapped and is being watched. She has been ordered to kill whoever befriends her and takes her in ... and that means our hero.

If she fails to kill him, the kidnappers will kill her. But if she kills him they'll let her go – or at least that's what they say. She thanks him for the tea, tells him he's a good man, and is full of apologies as she pulls out a gun and points it at his head.

How will he get out of this? How will he save the woman and bring the kidnappers to justice? If you can come up with a plausible solution, you're well on your way to a fantastic story.

If you can't think of any way of doing it, try getting together with some friends – and a few drinks – and see what you can come up with as a group.

> **[A possible solution]** My solution would be that there's someone else in the house – perhaps the man's wife – who could hit the woman and disarm her. They could then phone a neighbor, take her up into their roof-space and crawl along it to the neighbor's house. The neighbor is waiting for them, and he conceals the woman in his car, which is parked in his garage, and drives her away, perhaps to the train station.
>
> Of course, the villains are watching the couple's house, and they'll want the woman back. When she doesn't come out, they might break in and tear the place apart looking for her. So that's another problem the couple need to deal with. Perhaps one of them could call the police while they're shifting her through the roof-space. But, as this is a thriller, it won't be as easy as that!
>
> And there might be a further complication. The neighbor they're taking her to might be three or four houses away. The last time they checked their roof-space, it was possible to access the entire row of houses. But they haven't been up there for a while. And now they

discover that one of their other neighbors has built a wall up there. Their escape route is blocked.

81. Storyline: killing the tail

A killer has been arrested, but the police have had to release him because of a lack of evidence. Are they just going to let him disappear? Not likely! They're expecting new, conclusive evidence to come in at any moment, and they'll want to know exactly where he is when it arrives. So, naturally enough, they're going to follow his every move.

What if the killer finds out about this? He won't be happy. He might argue that it's an infringement of his civil liberties. But the police could counter-argue that he's a known security risk, so they're well within their rights. What will he do next?

He's killed at least once before, so perhaps he thinks it's time he did it again. If he got away with it once, then surely he can get away with it a second time?

Perhaps he's a member of a gang, and the other members spot that he's being tailed and let him know. If the other gang members have had run-ins with the police, they might be happy to help. They might even "eliminate" the officers who are following their comrade.

How will they do that? A quick drive-by shooting? Kidnap? Ambush? You could use any method you like. What's your favorite sort of crime? Or what crime would you most like to write about?

Is this the end for the officers on surveillance duty? It will be if the gang members have their way. Can the officers escape with their lives? What if they can't? What will happen next?

Lots to think about there, but it should lead to a thrilling story.

82. Storyline: Mafia forest fires

This story is based on a real incident. The Italian Government blamed the Mafia for starting hundreds of forest fires during hot, dry weather. Why did the Mafia do this? According to the Italian Government, Mafia companies would get the job of replanting all the forests, and the deforested areas could be used as landfill sites for dumping toxic waste.

This struck me as an excellent idea for a thriller. And since it's a real one, you can follow it in newspaper archives and online to see how it turned out in the end.

See if you can identify any strong characters among the government officials and politicians, Mafia members, reporters, fire officers, and forestry workers. Italian newspapers and websites will be a great source of information.

You could also see if you can find people who know more about the story than was reported in the media. For example, someone might have written about it in a blog post or article online, or discussed it in a Facebook group. Could there be more to this story than the public has been led to believe?

Much of the information you need will be in Italian, of course. But that isn't a problem any more. If you visit an Italian website, particularly using the Chrome web browser, you'll see a pop-up box offering to translate it into English. It probably won't be a perfect translation, but you should be able to get the gist of it.

Another option is to copy the address of the page from the address bar at the top of your web browser, go to Google Translate

(translate.google.com) and paste it in there. It will be the same translation – it's just another way of getting to it, and works in any web browser, not just Chrome. Other translation services are available.

It's well worth keeping an eye on the media for incidents like this. There's always something going on somewhere, so you'll never be short of ideas.

Even better, search for information about the incident online, but add a phrase such as "why aren't they reporting this?" You'll often find extra information that people connected to the incident know about, but the media are keeping quiet. The media might have been ordered to keep it out of the news – and that could make an interesting sub-plot for your story. Why have they been ordered to keep it quiet? Who gave the order? What if they disobey it?

83. Storyline: man with rifle?

Imagine that you're walking along a long, straight road. In the distance you see a car pull up. The driver gets out and sets up a tripod. He slowly and deliberately assembles a rifle and mounts it on the tripod. He attaches telescopic sights, then loads it with ammunition. And then he points it at you.

Are you his intended victim, or is he waiting for someone else? Will he kill you anyway because of what you've just witnessed? Perhaps your nerve fails you, and when you've seen enough, you run off to report him to the police.

But did you *really* see what you think you saw? Your imagination might have been playing tricks on you. Imagine your embarrassment when you learn that he was a plain-clothes police officer setting up a mobile speed trap. Or a surveyor working on a road-widening scheme. Or something else that's entirely innocent and lawful.

On the other hand, since you're writing a thriller, it's likely that it really *was* a rifle, and what the guy was doing was most definitely *not* lawful.

But if the police don't believe you, perhaps it's because they're involved in it too...

84. Storyline: man-made hurricane

What if mankind experienced its worst-ever hurricane: a once-in-a-million-years super-hurricane? That's scary enough, but let's raise the stakes even more. What if it was caused by terrorists?

How? Well, the basic principle is: the warmer the sea, the bigger the hurricane. If the terrorists' demands aren't met, they could wait for a hurricane to approach from the right direction, then lay hundreds of sheets of black polythene on the surface of the sea. By doing this, they should be able to raise the temperature of the sea in the hurricane's path. And that will increase the strength of the hurricane. (I'm making this up, by the way. I have no idea if it would actually work. But it sounds plausible, doesn't it?)

So, the terrorists threaten various Caribbean nations, especially those with U.S. interests. They make their demands: money, the cessation of military activity, the release of prisoners, or whatever it is they want. When those demands aren't met, they put their plan to warm the sea into operation.

It might not work. Or someone might stop them before they do any damage. One or more of the countries they're blackmailing might give in to their demands.

But if they go ahead with their plan, and it works, millions of people, and perhaps several entire countries, could be wiped out.

Once the plan is in operation, the countries might notice the sea temperature rising and give in to their demands. But it might be too late. Even if they remove the black sheeting now, the terrorists might have already warmed the water enough to cause a disaster on an epic scale.

85. Storyline: medical thriller

A medical doctor learns that his wife is terminally ill. He knows of an experimental program that's testing a new treatment, and it could save her. But for some reason she doesn't qualify for the program – perhaps they live in the wrong state, or she's too ill. So he breaks the rules and finds a way of getting her into the program.

But getting her in is only part of the problem. Half of the patients in the program – the control group – will be given a placebo drug that won't have any effect on them. Our doctor needs to make sure his wife gets the real thing. And that calls for some more rule-breaking.

What if the drug is less effective than its developers hoped? What if it does more harm than good? What if he hears about another program that's testing a different drug and getting better results? He might pull her out of the first program, break the rules all over again to get her into the other one, and somehow cover up the fact that she was ever enrolled in the first one.

If anyone finds out he's doing this – and how he's doing it – he'll be in serious trouble. But not as much trouble as his wife, who soon discovers that these two experimental drugs should never be mixed.

Perhaps there's a small chance that the two drugs might work together to cure her. But their combined side-effects might be so severe that she has little hope of surviving. Even if she does survive, how much of her body or brain might have been damaged? Maybe she would have been better off if he'd just let her die.

> **[EXTENSION]** Taking things a stage further, he might decide to give her the treatment she needs, but which the medical staff are denying her. They're almost certainly denying her the treatment for a good reason – but it might just be that it's too expensive.
>
> So he might remove her from the hospital, steal or borrow the drugs and equipment he needs, perhaps enlist the help of a few colleagues who owe him a favor, and carry out some illegal surgery. It's all pretty hopeless, but it's her only chance, so he feels he has no choice. He'll just have to deal with the consequences later: theft, illegal surgery, forged documents, deliberately giving false information on medical reports, and so on.
>
> **[VARIATIONS]** The doctor could be female and the sick person could be her husband. Or the sick person might be a lover (perhaps a secret one), child, mother, or someone else he or she cares deeply about – a famous actor, singer, writer, poet or athlete, for example.

86. Storyline: no more shaving

It begins innocently enough. A scientist, sick of having to shave every day, invents a new hair-removal product for men. You just slap it on your face, wait a few seconds, wash it off, and the job is done. It's tremendously popular.

Unfortunately, no one has realized that water doesn't stop it – it keeps on working. It builds up in your tissues over a period of weeks and months. People begin to notice side-effects. It doesn't just dissolve facial hair, it destroys other hair too. And then fingernails. And, eventually, it eats away at your bones.

The scientist tested the product on himself, and has therefore been using it for longer than anyone else. That means he's the first to notice the problems. It might start with a strange tingling sensation in his fingers and on his face. His hair starts to fall out – though he might assume that's just nature, because he's at that sort of age. Some of his fingernails look a little ragged, and they seem to have stopped growing. Then a couple of might them fall out. His doctor thinks it might be some sort of fungus, or maybe a thyroid problem. He prescribes him some drugs to treat it, but, of course, they make no difference.

He might accidentally hit his head on something – not particularly hard – but his skull or his jawbone fractures. And it won't heal. In fact, his bones are turning brittle and powdery. It isn't long before the bones at the ends of his fingers have been eaten away and they've become floppy and useless.

By the time he and his doctors have connected all of these problems to his hair-removal product, it might have been on the market for months. Millions of people might be using it.

Stores might be ordered to pull it from their shelves immediately. But, since there's no cure, they might decide not to alert the public. There's no point in worrying them. After all, they'll find out for themselves soon enough.

You could end the story there, or you could continue it as scientists race to find a cure or some way of reversing the effects. How long might that take? A year? Ten years? Thirty years? Longer? How many people die?

87. Storyline: quizmaster

An evil villain has captured a large group of people and locked them in a room which contains nothing but a television. One by one, each member of the group is taken into a separate room, asked questions by a quizmaster, and made to solve puzzles and riddles. If they get a question or puzzle wrong, they're immediately executed – and the rest of the group sees it happening on the TV. Then the next person is taken into the room, and the process is repeated.

Each person might be asked exactly the same set of questions and given the same set of puzzles and riddles to solve. Each time they answer a question correctly, they light up a square on a chart. At the top of the chart is the word "Freedom." Whenever someone answers a question wrongly, they're executed and all the lights on the chart go out. The next person has to start from scratch again. Everyone watching the TV can see how much progress has been made, what questions have been asked so far, and what the answers to those questions are. The question is, how cool can they remain under such pressure? How good will their memories be when they've just seen their friends die?

If the person currently being questioned believes in the afterlife, he might consider that he'd be better off dead anyway. In fact, he might be looking forward to seeing his dead friends and relatives again. So he might not be too concerned about getting a question wrong. But how will the rest of the group feel about that? They need his help. They need him to get the quizmaster to reveal the next set of questions.

What happens if someone eventually manages to answer all of the questions, and solve all the puzzles, and moves the light to the top of the chart? Will they *really* be set free? And if they are, will the rest of the group be set free too, or just that one person?

Perhaps those who remain will still have to answer all of the questions to win their freedom. And perhaps, once someone gets to the top of the chart and wins their freedom, the quizmaster might start afresh with a whole new set of questions and puzzles. Dozens more people might die before the next person wins their freedom.

Who is the mysterious quizmaster? Is he working alone, or does he belong to some sort of evil organization? What is his aim? Why has he come up with such an elaborate scheme? And who are the members of the group? How and why were they captured?

Answer these questions and you'll have a fantastic thriller.

88. Storyline: radar gun

A villainous electrical engineer realizes that he could adapt an old police radar gun into something that will kill people at a distance, without him getting caught. It should be particularly effective on people with heart pacemakers.

Does he target people that he knows have pacemakers? Or does he fire it at people randomly, occasionally catching those with pacemakers and killing them? Does it have any effect on those without pacemakers? Does it cause other electronic equipment they're carrying – such as mobile phones – to explode?

Why is he doing this? For the thrill of it? How does he avoid getting caught? Perhaps he hides himself well, or fires it from windows or from behind hedges, choosing his position carefully, so he won't be seen. As far as anyone is aware, the poor victim just collapses in front of them. It looks like a heart attack or seizure.

Our evil villain might have a job that takes him all over the country. He might have the ambition to kill one person in every county – and, eventually, in every town. He might chart them all on a map on his wall at home.

Will the police realize what's going on? Do they think these people are having genuine accidents or seizures or heart attacks, or that their pacemakers or phones are faulty? Will the manufacturers of these products get the blame? Will they have to pay out so much compensation that it puts them out of business? Or will the police realize there's an actual villain at work? Perhaps only one officer believes this, and he has to convince his skeptical colleagues and seniors. How might they go about catching the villain? How can they predict where and when he might strike next?

89. Storyline: reality TV

A family is being filmed for a TV series. I'll let you decide what the show is all about. What gets shown on TV is, of course, heavily edited. But what the audience doesn't know is that the family is being blackmailed, and perhaps even held against their will, by the TV producers.

As time goes on, the amount of footage they can broadcast becomes less and less, as much of it reveals what's really going on. The family might make various attempts to communicate with the outside world. Some of their messages might be subtle enough or cryptic enough to slip through the editing process – especially as the editors are running out of usable material and are getting desperate.

The 24-hour live feed that was being shown to paying subscribers has been cut off because it "wasn't getting enough viewers." And the daily or weekly highlights show is getting shorter and shorter (or they might pad it out with repeated clips, celebrity guests, and pseudo-psychological analysis) because there's so little footage they can actually broadcast.

Meanwhile, the family is trapped in a nightmare from which there seems to be no escape. Will anyone decode their secret messages? Will anyone come and save them? And why are the TV producers so evil?

90. Storyline: revenge of the spirit

Once someone has been killed, that's usually the last we hear from them. But not in this case. This is one angry and determined victim, and being dead has done nothing to cool his temper. In spirit form, he launches a three-pronged attack: haunting his killer, leaving messages for the detectives investigating the case, and passing messages to everyone else who might listen, including spirit mediums and clairvoyants, journalists, and so on.

Every time someone holds a ghost hunt or a vigil or a séance, regardless of where it's taking place, he hijacks it and tries to get his message across.

Ghost hunters soon become weary of this, and keep urging the police to arrest the villain. The police are being bombarded with information from just about every medium and clairvoyant in the country. Unfortunately, they can't use much of it because it isn't "direct evidence" and the courts won't accept it.

Meanwhile, the villain is beginning to rue the day he killed this particular victim. The ghost is driving him mad with all his hauntings and other bizarre happenings. He doesn't dare sleep because of the nightmares he keeps having. He's had the police on his doorstep more times than he can remember. And they've taken him to the police station for questioning many times too. At home, things disappear as soon as he turns his back on them, and he often finds weird, creepy things left in their place.

What sort of revenge does the victim want? Will he get it? Will the police finally get a piece of direct evidence they can actually use? Will it stand up in court? Will it be enough to convict the villain? Or will the villain crack under the pressure, hand himself in, and confess to the murder before that even happens?

Perhaps the only direct evidence the police have is somewhat flimsy, but it's still enough to get the villain to confess when they present him with it. By this stage, he'll do anything to get out of his house.

But will the hauntings stop when he's is in prison? Or will they continue, and eventually drive him out of his mind?

91. Storyline: special powers

A character with special powers is helping the intelligence services. For example, he might be telepathic. But details of his powers are leaked, and now subversive forces are out to get him. How does the information get leaked? Who leaks it, and why? What happens to the character?

Perhaps he knows the subversive forces are coming for him, and he helps set a trap to capture them. But, since this is an exciting thriller, something is bound to go wrong. What might that be?

92. Storyline: spores

When a botanist returns from an uninhabited tropical island with a beautiful new species of flowering plant, everybody wants one.

Luckily it grows well, and cuttings taken from it quickly take root and thrive. It soon becomes one of the most popular plants in the country.

Nothing untoward happens during the first year or two as the plants settle into their new environment. But once they're firmly established, something terrible happens. They release billions of spores that cause dangerous allergic reactions. With the plants now so widespread, the spores are everywhere – there's no escape. Millions of people become seriously ill, and hundreds, perhaps thousands, die. The country's healthcare system is unable to cope and grinds to a halt – with terrible consequences.

It certainly explains why the island was uninhabited. Perhaps the botanist was warned not to go there, but he went anyway. But why do these plants only seem to harm humans? They don't seem to be releasing the spores for breeding purposes or in self-defense – they seem to be launching a deliberate attack.

Why might this be to the plant's advantage? Perhaps the spores need to be buried deep underground to germinate. Since we bury our dead, the plants might have evolved to infect us with their spores and kill us. (Well that's my suggestion. Can you come up with a better one?)

The authorities order everyone to get rid of their plants as quickly as possible. Officials in protective suits go from door to door, collecting them and taking them away to be incinerated. Those who have been infected have to be kept in isolation in hospital, as the spores reproduce inside them. Whenever they exhale, they infect more people.

It will be too late for many people. There's a strong possibility that the whole country might have been infected. It might only be a matter of time before the entire population is wiped out. And other countries may have been infected too, by infected people traveling abroad or by people sending cuttings as gifts.

Scientists urgently need to develop some sort of decontamination process; something that will kill off the spores that are reproducing inside people. They also need to develop an antidote to combat all the other effects: the allergic reaction that no one is immune from, respiratory shutdown, and, ultimately, death.

The race is on. And the scientists have, of course, been infected too. So if they fail, they die. And so does everyone else.

> **[NOTE]** Australia bans the importation of plant material, so they might be the only country that's safe. Or at least they think they are. But infected people have been visiting the country for months, and infecting others.

> **[EXTENSION]** For a sci-fi thriller, what if the plants are an alien species? How did they get here? Can the spores travel through space? Were they dormant on Mars, but we brought back a soil sample, discovered them, and cultivated them to see what would happen?

93. Storyline: spurned lover

This story begins as a straightforward romance: girl meets boy, girl loses boy, girl wants boy back, but he's gone off with someone else.

In a regular romance, the girl would set about trying to win the boy back. But this is a thriller, and she doesn't want him back – she wants revenge!

What form her revenge takes is up to you. If you need some ideas, she could target her ex-boyfriend's new partner by doing things like:

- sabotaging her career
- throwing bricks through her windows
- setting her car on fire
- causing mysterious "accidents"
- and so on

Her ex-boyfriend and his new partner might know she's doing it, but they have no proof. Some of the accidents might even be genuine, but they can't be completely sure.

Then things go quiet for a while. They think she's finally come to terms with the situation, and they hope they'll be left in peace now. But they're wrong. She was just biding her time, making them sweat, or perhaps collecting the bits and pieces she needed for a bigger assault. She's tried all the obvious things to break them up, and they didn't work. So now the new girlfriend will have to die – and perhaps her ex-boyfriend too if he happens to be in the wrong place at the wrong time.

> [ALTERNATIVE 1] In the version above, she focuses on the new girlfriend. But you could write a version where she takes revenge on her ex-boyfriend instead. She might try to destroy him, or destroy his reputation or career, or ruin his life.
>
> [ALTERNATIVE 2] Or perhaps she goes after both of them. Maybe she alternates between them, or picks on whoever is the easiest target.

94. Storyline: the best detective

Who's the best detective in the city? That's what the people in this story aim to find out. They arrange for all the detectives they can find to work on the same case, without telling them that the others are working on it too.

It might not even be a real case, but an elaborate game. Perhaps it was set up by a TV company as a new reality show. As far as the detectives are concerned, it's totally real – they don't know what's really going on, and they don't suspect anything. They might be followed everywhere by members of the production team with hidden cameras. Points might be awarded at various stages: the first one to find the hidden evidence, interview the right witnesses, identify the main suspect, and so on. Bonus points might be awarded if they avoid the red herrings and traps or seduce the femme fatale. Points might be deducted when they make mistakes, cheat, or break the law.

At some point, the detectives will be told they're in a competition or game. Or perhaps they work it out for themselves. How you reveal it to them is up to you. Perhaps some of them have started following each other, believing that they're the suspects.

Those who score the most points might be invited to compete in a second round to win a major prize. This time there might be no rules or restrictions. All they have to do is solve the crime in the quickest time and score the most points along the way. But, of course, no one tells them how to score those points – that would make things too easy.

So now the real game begins, and this time they know they're competing against each other. And the prize is well worth winning. Over the next few days, weeks or months – or however long the contest runs for –

they'll try to outdo each other, cripple each other's chances, plant false evidence, set traps for each other, and so on.

I see this as a comedy-thriller, but you could leave out the comedy in your version if you prefer, and perhaps make it darker and more psychological.

95. Storyline: the enemy within

Tell the story of someone who is working for the state, perhaps as part of a security or military organization. But it gradually dawns on him that the people he's working for are not the decent, upright citizens he thought they were. The state is corrupt, the public is being fed false information, and news footage is being faked.

Our hero doesn't like this and turns against his employers. He's dedicated the best years of his life to safeguarding his country, but now he wants to destroy it – or at the very least take out those responsible for the corruption. And that basically amounts to the same thing. Our hero becomes the villain, although he obviously doesn't see it that way. He's out to destroy the state. And, once they realize this, the state is out to destroy *him*.

During his many years of service, he learned how the security forces operate, and that gives him a massive head start. He also has a wide network of military contacts, at home and abroad. His employers don't know about some of these people. In fact, they'd be shocked if they knew who he was on first name terms with.

It's going to be a thrilling and challenging battle – and a great story. But who will win? Our hero-villain might not manage to overthrow the state, but he might end the careers – and lives – of some of the most corrupt people running it.

Will someone finally stop him? How far will he manage to get? What if they can't stop him? What will happen to him if he's caught?

96. Storyline: triple paranoia

Our hero insists that someone is out to get him. But no one takes his claim seriously. He might have had similar episodes before; everyone thinks the poor guy is deluded. But he is right, and they are wrong: someone really *is* out to get him. They might have been making attempts on his life for months or years. Our poor hero isn't so paranoid after all.

But when he arrives home one day, bleeding heavily from a head wound, his family decides that enough is enough. He's obviously so deranged that he's started harming himself just to get attention. Ignoring his claims that he's been attacked again, they drive him to the nearest secure mental hospital and have him admitted for his own safety.

But this particular hospital is testing experimental treatments. Not only are they trying out new techniques, they're also re-evaluating some of the more horrific ones from the past. And our hapless hero is the perfect candidate for their research.

He doesn't know any of this, of course. In fact, he's happy to be in the hospital, because it's a secure building and he should be safe from his tormentors.

But then the experiments begin. He soon realizes what's going on. He's in a dangerous predicament, and he needs to get out of there.

Somehow, he manages to escape. But the police and health authorities are now out to get him, as well as the people who were after him in the first place. The media reports that a dangerous lunatic is on the run from the asylum. So now his tormentors know he's no longer in safe custody. And that means they can make yet another attempt to kill him.

His chances of escaping from this three-pronged attack are slim-to-none. But that's what makes it such a terrific story.

97. Storyline: two in one

During a routine investigation, a body is exhumed from a grave. To everyone's astonishment, when the casket is opened there are two bodies inside. Several people went missing in the area recently, and the second body turns out to be one of them.

The police order all recently buried caskets to be exhumed. The families they belong to will of course protest and make things as difficult as possible for them. But, sure enough, several of those caskets contain extra bodies too.

But how did they get there? Where they added at the mortuary? Or were the caskets dug up after being buried, and then reburied with the extra body inside? It's all very mysterious.

Now let's add the thriller aspects. Imagine that during the investigation one of the police officers goes missing. Everyone immediately assumes the worst – that he'll turn up in one of the caskets. But since the case was made public, no further caskets have been buried, and the police have been keeping a 24-hour watch on all the mortuaries and cemeteries in the area. Or so they think...

Despite their hard work, one more body slips through their net. How? Well, the police failed to consider one vital aspect. But what is it?

Perhaps the villain wants to demonstrate how smart he is. As soon the police allow burials to proceed again, the villain calls them to say there's an extra body in one of the newly buried caskets. The police have been monitoring things and assume it's a hoax. But imagine their surprise when they discover there really is an extra body.

The body wasn't the missing officer, but a race now begins to try and find him. They also need to work out how the villain is still managing to get extra bodies into the caskets, and how to prevent him from killing anyone else. And every casket that was buried recently – including all of the ones they thought they were keeping an eye on – will have to be exhumed and checked.

Now let's raise the stakes even further by having a second officer go missing. Do either (or both) of these officers turn up alive or dead? That's for you to decide. How about if they're put into the caskets alive, but with a limited air supply? Perhaps the villain sends the police a note telling them this, but he doesn't say which grave or which cemetery they're buried in.

We now have a life-or-death story with a time limit – a classic thriller technique.

98. Storyline: ultimate revenge

Write the story of someone who feels he's been wronged by his state or country and decides to take the ultimate revenge by destroying it.

Perhaps, when his initial complaints are ignored, he contacts the President or Prime Minister or the monarch. But when he receives no response, or a standard reply that shows they don't care, he starts to cause real damage.

He might:

- poison food and water supplies
- shut down cooling and safety systems at nuclear power stations, either during a guided tour or by hacking into their systems remotely
- make accusations against foreign powers in an attempt to provoke sanctions or war
- leak state secrets
- cause train or plane crashes and blame them on foreign powers or terrorists, perhaps causing all planes to be grounded for months
- cause multiple car crashes that gridlock all the major roads
- provoke national strikes
- and so on

Intelligence agents will undoubtedly identify him as the culprit or main suspect, but it's up to you to decide how quickly they do this. They'll then follow him and monitor his communications to prevent him from causing any more damage. But there might still be occasions when he slips through their net.

Some of the issues he sets in motion might be (almost) unstoppable. The authorities might have a limited amount of time to put right the damage, prevent disaster, restore relationships with other countries, and so on. They might not always succeed.

What happens to him in the end? Was his initial complaint justified? Will it ever be addressed? Or will he just find something else to complain about?

99. Storyline: villains everywhere

Wherever our hero goes, he meets the villain and his henchmen. If he takes a taxi cab or a bus, the villain or one of his employees is driving it. If he goes into a store, the person who serves him is a member of the villain's team – and so is the store detective. If he tries to buy or rent a house, the realtor is on the villain's side too – as are all the tradesmen who visit.

But is that *really* the case? Maybe he only suspects they're connected to the villain, but he can't prove it. Is he just being paranoid? Perhaps he needs to see a psychologist. But if he does, won't the psychologist be one of the villain's henchmen too – or even the villain himself? (Or at least that's what our unfortunate hero suspects.)

Big Brother is always watching. But Big Brother only seems to be watching *him*. And this Big Brother is evil.

So what's really going on? Is he the victim of an elaborate prank? Or is something more sinister happening?

100. Storyline: war: a diplomatic solution

Our hero tries to prevent a war between two countries. As tensions on both sides escalate, he travels the world trying to gain support for a diplomatic solution. He often finds himself thwarted by countries that have arranged military and arms deals with one side or the other (sometimes both). They'll make a handsome profit if the war goes ahead. Other countries just don't want to get involved.

It looks as if his attempts at diplomacy are doomed to failure. Is there any way he can prevent the war from going ahead with a last-minute intervention? Or will he become the first casualty of the conflict?

101. Storyline: war: a presidential solution

The next presidential election is coming up. Concerned that his country is heading towards a war it can't possibly win, the hero of this story does everything in his power to get himself elected. He will then withdraw the country's troops.

If the war goes ahead, thousands of people will be killed or injured, and the economy will be devastated. He's determined to prevent any of that from happening – but perhaps not for the reasons he claims.

Perhaps his own business interests would suffer if the war went ahead. Perhaps he has relatives or business partners in the country they're going to war with. He'll probably want to keep quiet about that.

To get elected as president, he's going to need funding (a lot), training, and advisers. He'll need to come across as being friendlier, more honest, more ethical, and more competent than all of the other candidates. And he'll need to choose the right political party to join – or at least the one that has the most public support – even if he hates what that party stands for.

Unfortunately, the party with the most public support is the one that wants the war to go ahead. So, for the duration of his campaign, he'll have to support the "wrong" side – or at least give the appearance of doing so.

He'll do whatever it takes to get elected, including lying and cheating and all sorts of other dirty tricks. Because it's all in a good cause and it's what's best for the country.

As is the case with several of the storylines we've discussed, this one would work well as a comedy-thriller. Or you could leave out the comedy and explore the darker side of politics. Either way, you won't be short of material. Just refer back to the media coverage of the last election.

102. Storyline: whatever it takes

A lowly employee in a large organization is determined to reach the top and become its chief executive as quickly as possible. He has big plans for the company, and he'll do whatever it takes to get there. He's absolutely ruthless. If he has to force those above him to quit, get them fired, have them killed, make them retire on health grounds, get them pregnant, write fake reports in their name, send fake emails, circulate fake photos, and otherwise ruin their reputations and careers, that's all fine by him. It's all part of the game. In fact, it's more than fine: it's also brilliant fun. Until …?

> [EXTENSION] Once he gets to the top, he might decide to take over other companies by using the same methods. Again, he'll be brutal and mercenary about it, and he takes no prisoners.
>
> He'll get his comeuppance in the end, of course – and then some. But he'll destroy more than a few people and businesses along the way.

About the Author

Dave Haslett won his first writing competition at the age of seven. The prize was a Spirograph art set, which he loved, even though he wasn't very good at it.

He then set up his own home aquarium. Not having much money, and finding the books on the subject at his local library somewhat lacking, he set about writing his own hand-illustrated encyclopedia of freshwater tropical fish. It took him nearly two years to complete, and he finished it when he was thirteen. It still looks impressive forty years later.

Always an avid reader, he was delighted when the county library service launched a contest based on the number of books people read. (You had to answer questions to prove you'd read them.) He became the first in the county to reach the target, and was presented with a shield and a certificate by a famous athlete he'd never heard of – although his mother seemed rather impressed. He was also featured in the local newspaper – the first of many appearances. They said he preferred books to TV. But that wasn't the case at all – they never even asked him about that!

An unfortunate side-effect of reading so many books in such a short time was that he'd exhausted the library's stock. They had nothing worth reading that he hadn't read already. He began cycling four miles to the next one, but it was only a little library, and he'd soon exhausted their stock too. So what now? Start writing his own, of course!

Blessed with far more ideas than he could ever use, even in several lifetimes, he launched the ideas4writers website in 2002, so he could share them with those who needed them. He soon amassed a collection of well over 5,000 ideas. He has now repackaged these into a series of books, each devoted to a single genre or topic. And you're reading one of them right now! If you thought it was good, please do him a favor and leave a review on Amazon - thanks!

The ideas4writers website is still active, but it now focuses on author services, including editing, proofreading, ghostwriting, audio transcriptions, book layouts and formatting, and cover design.

If you're in need of any of these, please take a look at www.ideas4writers.co.uk or email dave@ideas4writers.co.uk

30936515R00068

Printed in Great Britain
by Amazon